The Essence of Consumer Behaviour

PUBLISHED TITLES

The Essence of Consumer Behaviour

Jim Blythe

Prentice Hall

London   New York   Toronto   Sydney   Tokyo   Singapore
Madrid   Mexico City   Munich   Paris

First published 1997 by
Prentice Hall Europe
Campus 400, Maylands Avenue
Hemel Hempstead
Hertfordshire, HP2 7EZ
A division of
Simon & Schuster International Group

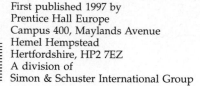

Typeset in 10/12 pt Palatino
by Photoprint, Torquay, Devon

Printed and bound in Great Britain by
Hartnolls Limited, Bodmin, Cornwall

Library of Congress Cataloging-in-Publication Data

Available from the publisher

British Library Cataloguing in Publication Data

A catalogue record for this book is available from
the British Library

ISBN 0-13-356502–5

1   2   3   4   5   01   00   99   98   97

To Sue, with love

Contents

Introduction: The importance of understanding consumer behaviour

> People who understand consumer behaviour make more money in the stock market than professional stock pickers who rely on financial numbers. 'If you like the store, chances are you'll love the stock'.
>
> Peter Lynch[1]

After reading this introduction, you should be able to:

- Explain the role consumer behaviour has within the marketing concept.
- Define the main concepts of consumer behaviour.
- Explain the role of relationship marketing.

Consumers and the marketing concept

In its most basic form, the marketing concept states that organizations need to anticipate and satisfy consumer needs if they are to remain on top in terms of making profits. Marketing is about ensuring that whatever the firm does is done with consumers in mind. The following quotes illustrate this.

> Without customers, there *is* no business. (Anon.)

> The sole purpose of a business is to create a customer. (Peter Drucker, management guru)

> The customer is always right; and even if the customer is wrong, he's still the customer. (Sign seen in a sports shop in Somerset)

1

The marketing concept is important because consumers have very wide choice as to where to spend their hard-earned money. People are better educated than ever before, with greater spending power and mobility, and they are able to shop around much more in order to buy whatever best meets their needs. If there is room for four companies in a given market, five companies will be in there competing for survival; in that situation, the consumer is king. Far from choosing from what you have to offer, the modern consumer will tell you what he or she wants, and if you cannot supply it, your competitors will.

The marketing concept therefore requires that managers observe everything from the viewpoint of the consumer; look at the firm and its products as the consumer sees them; and plan around the consumer's needs and aspirations.

An example of this in the USA comes from the Wal-Mart chain of hardware shops. Wal-Mart's Sam Walton (founder of the company) says he acts 'as an agent for his retail customers'. In other words, he sees his role as being to find out what his customers want to buy, and then to go out to the manufacturers and wholesalers and buy the products on their behalf. Of course, Wal-Mart operates like any other retail outlet, in that the goods are displayed on the shelves for customers to come in and buy; but the difference lies in the philosophy behind Sam Walton's approach. Wal-Mart is now the largest retailer in the USA, with sales of over $32 billion per annum.[2]

An example of similar thinking in the UK comes from Boot's the chemists. The founder of the company, Jesse Boot, would regularly go into his shops and demand, 'What have you got for a penny!' He was well aware that his customers were often poor people who would be unable to buy a whole bottle of aspirins, so he insisted that his managers sold perhaps a few pills for a penny. As a wheelchair user himself due to long-term illness, Boot understood his customers' needs and responded to them. The company has grown to the extent that 40 per cent of British women now visit Boot's in any one week.

Consumer behaviour has been described as 'the dynamic interaction of affect and cognition, behaviour, and environmental events by which human beings conduct the exchange aspects of their lives' (American Marketing Association). Since this statement is somewhat lengthy and complex, it may be useful to break it down and define some of the terms.

● *Consumer behaviour is dynamic* – changing and evolving. This means that many statements about consumer behaviour will, eventually, become irrelevant as fashions in thought and social conditions change. Even the briefest examination of human cultures worldwide will show that there are very few absolute rules to human behaviour, and that new ideas and approaches are constantly being adopted.

- *Consumer behaviour involves interactions*: we need to know what consumers think (*cognition*), what they feel (*affect*), what they do (*behaviours*) and the things and places that influence and are influenced by what they think, feel and do (*environment*). Clearly thoughts and emotions colour behaviour; but behaviour itself leads to other, related, behaviour. For example, if somebody goes skiing this leads to other behaviour – buying clothing, buying ski equipment, buying air tickets, buying drinks in the bar 'après-ski', and so forth. Likewise, getting drunk leads to buying hangover cures, and making friends leads to buying birthday cards.

- *Consumer behaviour involves exchanges* between human beings. Trade can only happen when *both* parties end up better off; if this were not so, people would not want to trade. For example, a consumer going to the pub would rather have the beer than the money it costs to buy it, but the landlord would rather have the money than the beer. By the end of the evening, both parties feel considerably better off as a result of the transactions. From the landlord's viewpoint, of course, it is worthwhile ensuring that the customer enjoys not only the beer but the whole experience of the pub (the atmosphere, the service, perhaps the music or the food). This is because a small group of 'regulars' will be worth more in the long run than a large group of casual or occasional customers.

Behaviour is therefore the result of a complex interaction of many factors, most of which will vary from one individual to the next.

Consumers and the four Ps

The classical view of strategic marketing is that it involves decisions concerning the four Ps: product, place, price and promotion. Subsequently, this list has been expanded by Booms and Bitner[3] to include people, physical evidence and processes – and indeed Wind[4] has suggested that the marketing mix contains a total of eleven elements.

Much marketing activity is actually product orientated: that is to say, the company focuses on the product's characteristics rather than the consumer's characteristics. At the extreme, the company produces a product which the engineers and accountants believe is the best that can be made for the price, yet which has no relevance to consumers' needs. The drawback of this approach is that the consumer is unlikely to buy a product which does not meet a need, and will not respond to advertising that does not appeal.

If marketers are to take a truly consumer-orientated view within the basic four Ps structure, they would need to ask themselves questions along these lines:

- *Product*. What products are the consumers using at present? What do they like about the products, and what don't they like about them? What would they like the products to do, in addition to what they do already?
- *Place*. Where would they like to buy our product from? Where do they currently buy this type of product, and why? Is it convenient for them to buy from this source? Could we make it easier for them to buy our product by offering it through a different outlet?
- *Price*. What price will they see as good value? This is not necessarily the lowest price; very few consumers (if any) consistently buy the cheapest products they can find. However, most have a very clear idea of what represents good value for money.
- *Promotion*. What type of promotion will interest them? Which will encourage them to buy? Which addresses their needs, in terms of activating the need and offering a credible way of satisfying it?

Essentially, this approach means starting with the consumer when faced with any marketing question. The problem here is that there is no such thing as 'the consumer'; there are only people who have differing needs and interests. Therefore marketers try to group consumers into *segments* with similar needs and desires; this makes it easier to answer the questions above. A market segment might comprise people who live in the same area, or who have similar behaviour patterns, or who are of a similar age. In other words, consumer-orientated marketers will try to get a clear mental picture of their typical or best customers and try to fit the company's activities to those customers.

It follows that the study of how those consumers behave, and how they are likely to respond to our activities, is crucially important if we are to be successful in marketing. In practice, many firms ignore the consumer, and indeed much effort and many resources are wasted because of this. For example, a study carried out on 11,000 new products launched by 77 different companies found that, five years later, only 56 per cent were still on the market. This means that almost half the products had to be withdrawn, presumably because consumers just did not want to buy them in sufficient numbers to make it worth keeping them in production.[5]

An understanding of consumers, and a customer-orientated approach, is important to any firm seeking to succeed in a competitive environment, but understanding consumer behaviour is not straightforward. Some of the problems with understanding consumers are as follows:

- They are all different.
- They often act emotionally rather than rationally.
- They act differently at different times and often respond differently to the same stimulus at different times.

- They can be persuaded – by you, and by your competitors. In other words, they learn, and thereby change their attitudes and behaviour.

Consumer research is sometimes difficult and usually costly, which is another reason why firms often do not bother to do it. On the other hand, the cost of doing consumer research pales into insignificance against the cost of not doing it, as the example of Sir Clive Sinclair's C5 electric vehicle illustrates.

Sir Clive Sinclair is a highly intelligent electronics expert who was responsible for developing a huge range of innovative electronic devices. During the 1960s he designed and marketed a wrist radio and a series of self-assembly kits for the electronics enthusiast; during the early 1970s he helped develop the electronic calculator, and he marketed an early form of personal computer, the ZX80, long before the major companies had made any serious inroads into the home computer market. His company also developed a miniature hand-held TV set using technology so advanced that when Binatone bought the rights to the design, it was unable to duplicate the design in its Japanese factories.

In 1984 Sinclair launched the C5, an ergonomically designed, one-person electric vehicle which was environmentally friendly, required no driving licence and could park almost anywhere with ease. By May 1985 Sinclair reported sales of 8,000 vehicles, but by October 1985 debts on the project had risen to £7.75 million and sales had all but ceased. The remaining vehicles had to be sold off at less than the cost of manufacture, and Sir Clive Sinclair virtually retired from industry.

The reasons for the failure of the C5 project have been debated endlessly, but at the end of the day there can be only one reason for the product's failure: consumers were not prepared to buy it. Had Sinclair carried out suitable consumer research, this problem might have come to light much earlier; any of the following conclusions might have emerged.

- The product might have been shown to have no substantial market at all, in which case it need not have gone into production.
- An alternative market might have been identified – for example, C5s have been used successfully in warehouses, private estates and leisure complexes.
- An alternative promotional strategy might have been devised. There is little doubt that the C5 was almost ridiculed off the market by the news media, since it was promoted as an electric car yet was only able to carry one person.

In fairness, of course, research is not perfect and sometimes the best research available still results in failures when the product reaches the market. But good research will improve the odds enormously.

Figure 1 Segmentation of the clothing market

Consumers and segmentation

Nowadays mass markets seldom exist. There are very few products that are bought by nearly everybody, simply because different consumers have different needs. Marketers group consumers with similar sets of needs into segments. As time goes by and research improves, it is becoming possible to segment markets into smaller and smaller groups. Figure 1 shows an example of how groupings can form in the clothing market.

The needs of each segment of the market will differ – teenagers have different clothing requirements from the older age groups – but even within the teenage segment there will be further groupings of needs. Street clothes will not be the same as disco/party wear for teenagers, and there will be further subgroupings. For example, within the 25 to 45 age group there will be divisions according to income, according to lifestyle, according to geographical area and according to social class.

Each group will need to be treated differently; each group will make choices that affect what they will buy, and where, and how much they will pay for it. Likewise, each group will respond to a different form of promotional activity. The kind of advertising that would appeal to teen-agers is unlikely to appeal to elderly people, so marketers will try to *target* these groups separately, and indeed target subgroups within these broad groupings.

The consumer and relationship marketing

Until recently, most marketers have really been concerned only with transactions. In some cases, notably in house sales, marketers have been concerned with single transactions; once the house is sold, there has been an assumption that that is the end of the consumer's interest in the developer, unless, of course, problems develop with the house.

Within the last five to ten years there has been a new emphasis on viewing the consumer as a long-term 'asset' of the business, rather than a one-off buyer. Companies have come to realize that it is much easier (and cheaper) to keep an existing customer than it is to attract a new one, and marketers have therefore been much concerned with establishing relationships with customers and consumers. Much of the work on relationship marketing has concentrated on the supply-chain relationships between manufacturers and intermediaries, but this is by no means the only application of the relationship marketing approach.

The essence of relationship marketing (as it applies to consumers) is to find out which customers are going to be of the most long-term value to the firm: that is to say, which ones are most likely to remain loyal. These customers are not necessarily the richest, or the biggest spenders; relationship marketing tells us that one customer who spends a regular £30 a month with us for twenty years is worth more than five customers who spend £500 with us once and are never heard from again. Consumers are therefore viewed as lifetime profit centres who may spend hundreds of thousands of pounds with us during a lifetime, rather than as sources of a one-off profit from one transaction.

This approach has only become possible due to the existence of sophisticated research tools and computerized systems by which consumers can be identified and categorized. Firms then seek to establish a longer-term rapport with the consumers to ensure loyalty.

An example is the frequent-flyer programmes initiated by the major airlines. Having identified that those who fly frequently for business purposes are also likely to fly for leisure activities, the airlines offer free leisure flights for those who fly frequently on business. Frequent flyers also receive special offers, free magazines with articles which are of interest to travellers, and discount vouchers for duty-free goods and hotels. This encourages the frequent flyers to fly with the same airline each time so as to accumulate the free gifts, but it also allows the airline to market other services to these customers. The discounted hotels, for example, are not actually free!

A second example is the growth in multilevel, or network, marketing. In multilevel marketing, or MLM, each consumer also acts as an agent for recruiting more consumers, earning a commission on each sale made to somebody else. This results in a classic pyramid structure, with each consumer selling to family and friends, and also recruiting family and friends into the network. The growth potential for such a network is huge, and since it relies on the relationships between the consumers/agents in the network, it will generate strong loyalty among consumers. Companies such as Amway have developed worldwide customer bases by creating such selling networks, and there are now many examples of MLM networks selling everything from household cleaning fluids to health foods.

The growth in relationship marketing is likely to be of benefit to consumers, since companies are going to great lengths to look after them and help meet their needs; many consumers are fickle, and need to be wooed by increasingly subtle means.

The consumer and marketing planning

Marketing is very much like buying a Christmas present for a family member; the comparison of the process is as shown in Table 1. Looked at in this way, it is easy to see where relationship marketing fits in. If you have a reputation for buying good, useful, interesting presents, people will look forward to your gifts and will try to please you in return. Exactly the same is true of marketing.

Ultimately, marketing is about meeting people's needs, and therefore the study of consumers and their needs is crucial to the study of marketing.

Table 1 Comparison of marketing with buying a present

Buying a present	Marketing
Decide who you are buying for.	Identify the target market.
Decide how much to spend – usually based on how much you expect them to spend on you!	Decide what price the customer is prepared to pay.
Think about the person's interests or needs.	Think about the consumer's interests and needs.
Look around for what's available within the price range, bearing in mind what the person would like.	Decide which features can be included within the price the consumer is prepared to pay.
Buy the present.	Launch the product.
Wrap the present.	Package the product.
Have it delivered/take it round.	Arrange a suitable distribution method.
Watch the person's face when they open it!	Get feedback from the customers after purchase.
Decide whether the present was *really* what the person wanted.	Carry out research to determine whether the product could be improved for next time.

Key points from the introduction

In this introduction we have taken a quick overview of consumer behaviour, and the reasons for studying it. Here are the main points:

- Consumer behaviour is the result of many factors, including affect, cognition, conation, environment and behaviour itself.
- Consumers are all different; they're a lot like people in that respect.
- Marketing is about finding out what people need and seeing that they get it, at a profit.
- Consumers can be grouped according to the similarity of their needs; these groupings are called segments.
- People only buy what they want to buy, and if you can't supply it, they will go to somebody who can.
- Consumer behaviour changes over time, so firms have to keep monitoring their customers to ensure that their needs are being met.
- If you ignore your customers, your customers will ignore you.

Notes

1. Peter Lynch, *Beating the Street* (New York: Simon and Schuster, 1993).
2. Bill Saporito, 'Is Wal-Mart unstoppable?', *Fortune*, 6 May 1991.
3. B.H. Booms and M.J. Bitner, 'Marketing strategies and organisation structures for service firms', in J. Donnelly and W.R. George (eds.), *Marketing of Services* (Chicago, IL: American Marketing Association, 1981).
4. Y. Wind, 'Models for marketing planning and decision-making', in V.P. Buell (ed.), *Handbook of Modern Marketing*, 2nd edn (New York: McGraw-Hill, 1986).
5. 'Flops', *Fitness Week*, 16 August 1993, p. 79.

1

Drive, motivation and hedonism

This chapter examines some of the theories of motivation that underpin the study of consumer behaviour. After reading the chapter, you should be able to:

- Explain the types of motive that cause people to buy.
- Describe the motivation theories of Maslow and Hertzberg.
- Show how the theories fit into the practicalities of consumer buying behaviour.
- Explain how needs become translated into wants, and how wants translate into action.

Classification of motives

Motives can be classified as shown in Table 1.1. Although it is difficult to separate out people's motivations for making particular purchases, it can be said with some certainty that the emotional and dormant motives often take precedence over the rational and conscious motives. For example, it is plainly foolish and dangerous to try bungee-jumping, and no rational reason exists for doing it, yet it is an immensely popular activity; it is fun and exciting, and tests the bravery of the participants. Likewise, fashion purchases are often impractical and overpriced, yet the emotional need of appearing fashionable overwhelms the rational, conscious motive of buying something to keep out the cold.

Motives should be distinguished from instincts. A motive is simply a reason for carrying out a particular behaviour; it is not an automatic response to a stimulus. Instincts are pre-programmed responses which are

10

Table 1.1 Classification of motives

Primary motives	The reason that leads to the purchase of a product *class*. For instance, a consumer may need to buy a car to replace an old, worn-out one.
Secondary motives	These are the reasons behind buying a particular *brand*. The consumer may have reasons for buying a Vauxhall rather than a Peugeot, or a Ford rather than a BMW.
Rational motives	Based on reasoning, or logical assessment of the consumer's situation. Our car purchaser may have worked out a need for a car that will carry four kids and a tent, and will base the choice on that.
Emotional motives	These motives have to do with the consumer's feeling about the brand. Our hypothetical car purchaser may end up buying a sports car despite the need for a car that will carry four kids and a tent!
Conscious motives	Motives of which the consumer is aware. Our car buyer *knows* he needs a new car, so this is a conscious motive.
Dormant motives	Motives operating below the conscious level. The hypothetical car buyer may not be aware that his desire for the sports car is linked to his approaching middle age.

inborn in the individual, and which are involuntary. Although behaviour may result from an instinctive source (for example, cinema-goers who are watching an IMAX or a three-dimensional film show may instinctively duck or gasp at a particularly dramatic moment), virtually all consumer behaviour is non-instinctive, or volitional.

Essentially, consumers are motivated by a desire to satisfy their needs. There are many ways of defining what constitutes a need, and probably in most people's minds the word is associated with the necessities of life: food, shelter and clothing. However, this definition is somewhat slippery, since human beings are complex creatures whose needs go beyond the merely physiological. For example, a human being who is deprived of social contact for a long period will eventually become insane; likewise, people have a need for sensory stimulation (entertainment). Marketers therefore define *need* as a *perceived lack*. This definition means that merely lacking something does not create a need, but the individual's realization that he or she lacks something means that the need has come into being. For example, a lack of snowshoes does not constitute a need unless there is heavy snow, and also a need to travel some distance on foot.

The sense of unease produced by an unfulfilled need causes a series of events to take place in the consumer's mind, as shown in Table 1.2. As the individual moves from one activity to another down the list, the behaviour becomes more specific and more observable: from a vague feeling that something is amiss, the consumer moves to the point of putting on a coat and stepping out to the chip shop. This sequence of thought will often occur within a very short space of time.

Table 1.2 Formation of goals and action

Psychological event	Explanation
Need is recognized.	The feeling of lacking something is categorized: for example, the consumer becomes aware that the feeling of unease is caused by hunger.
A drive is generated.	A desire to do something about the problem comes to mind.
A relevant motive is selected.	The consumer looks for something to eat.
A goal is selected.	Some specific food is aimed for; perhaps the individual decides to buy a take-away meal.
A pattern of action is selected to achieve the goal.	The consumer decides whether to go out and buy the food, or telephone for it to be delivered.

Felt needs can be classified into two broad categories: *utilitarian* needs, which lead the consumer to consider the objective, functional attributes of the product; and *hedonic* or *experiential* needs, which lead the consumer to consider the subjective, pleasurable or aesthetic aspects of the product.[1]

It is quite common for both types of need to be considered in the same purchase decision. A consumer may buy a car for the *utilitarian* purpose of driving to and from work, but decide to buy a sports car for the *experiential* purpose of enjoying the ride. In fact, Melvin Copeland[2] claimed in 1924 that consumers are motivated by both rational and emotional motives, and although there was a shift in emphasis during the 1960s and 1970s towards rational explanations for behaviour, the current view is that there is a balance between the two types of motive.[3]

A second definition that may be useful here is *want*. Again, a layperson's definition might be that a want is something inessential or unimportant. This is not a usable definition, since one person's luxury might be another person's necessity. For example, most people living in Britain would regard a refrigerator as a necessity, yet for most of the world's population it would be a real luxury. For reasons of clarity, therefore, marketers define a want as a *specific satisfier* for a need. For example, an individual might *need* food, but *want* a hamburger, or might *need* a drink but *want* beer.

There are many ways in which a given need can be satisfied. The need for companionship could be supplied by joining a club, or meeting up with some friends to go out somewhere, or going to the pub, or calling round to a friend's house for a coffee. Needs tend to be general, whereas wants are specific. Because of this, much marketing effort is expended on encouraging consumers to meet their needs with a specific satisfier (Thirsty? Drink cola!).

Figure 1.1 shows a model of motivation which develops from the sequence shown in Table 1.2. This model includes the factors of learning and expectancy. In the diagram, the unfilled need leads to the development

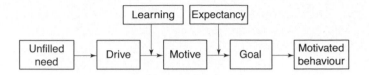

Figure 1.1 Motivation model (Source: Adapted from Sak Onkvisit and John J. Shaw, *Consumer Behaviour, Strategy and Analysis*, New York: Macmillan, 1994)

of a drive which must be fulfilled. The consumer's previous learning about what might be appropriate action leads to the development of a motive or series of motives; the consumer has expectations about what will happen as a result of acting on the motives, and from this formulates a goal. This in turn will lead to behaviour designed to achieve the goal.

This model tends to imply a very clear, rational approach to consumer behaviour. In fact, much of the processing that goes on in the model happens in the deep recesses of the consumer's brain, and would run on the lines of 'I'm thirsty. There's a Coke machine – I've had Coke before and liked it. Where's the 60p for the machine?' This often happens without conscious thought – sometimes as a result of seeing the Coke machine, which makes the consumer aware of a thirst that, until a few moments before, had been below the conscious level. Some of the ways in which the unconscious, or subconscious, mind operates are described in Chapter 3.

Drive

Drive is the force that makes a person respond to a need. It is an internal stimulus, and is caused by the drift from the *desired state* to the *actual state*. Drive is usually felt as tension, or restlessness.

If a gap opens up between where the person is now and where he or she would like to be, a drive to correct the situation is generated. The strength of the drive will depend on the size of the gap between the desired and actual states. For example, becoming thirsty leads to a drive to find something to drink; the thirstier one becomes, the greater the drive to have a drink. Once one has quenched the thirst, though, the tension disappears and the energy formerly devoted to finding a drink will become channelled elsewhere. From a marketer's viewpoint, the main way that drives can be generated is by encouraging a revision of the desired state: that is, getting the person to feel dissatisfied with the actual state.

If the drive state is at a high level, the individual is more open to suggestions about new ways of satisfying the need. Someone who is thirsty may be prepared to try a new soft drink if the usual brand is unavailable; somebody who is desperately hungry is more likely to be prepared to try an unusual food. Most people are familiar with the problems of food shopping when hungry; it is easy to overload the trolley with food, and one is often tempted to try new foods.

If the drive state is at a low level, the individual may still be stimulated into taking action by a reminder. For example, it is common to see signs saying 'Teas, Coffees, Sandwiches, Burgers 150 Yards' when driving. These signs give the motorist just enough time to think 'I could do with a cuppa' before the lay-by with the snack van in it appears.

The snack van owner would not have thought through the psychology of the sign, but on a simple level it works. This is called *activating a need*. Although the motorist is not actively looking for a cup of tea, the sign acts as a reminder that a cup of tea would be enjoyable. Motorists whose drive state is at zero (perhaps because they just had a cup of tea) will continue straight past, but the success rate of the signs is great enough to make it worthwhile setting them out each day.

It is, of course, stimulating and enjoyable to allow some gaps to develop between desired and actual states; this is what keeps life interesting for most people. Allowing oneself to grow hungry before going out for a meal, or working up a thirst before going to the pub, make the subsequent experiences more enjoyable. Likewise, achieving the desired state (for example, getting a promotion) may eventually lead to a raising of the individual's sights and a desire to go for an even higher grade of job. In consumer terms, somebody who has saved for years to buy a BMW may very well immediately start saving to buy an even more expensive BMW.

Each individual has a level at which this type of stimulation is enjoyable and challenging, without being uncomfortable or worrying. This is called the *optimum stimulation level* or OSL. If external stimulation goes above the optimum level, the individual will seek to satisfy the need and reduce the drive; if stimulation falls below the OSL, the individual will seek to increase the stimulation to bring it back up to the OSL.

The OSL is a subjective factor: that is to say, it varies from one individual to another. Research has shown that those with high OSLs like novelty and risk taking, whereas those with low OSLs prefer the tried and tested.[4] Those with high OSLs tend to be younger people.

Motivation in action

Motives are the reasons why people take action. A motive can have both strength and direction, and can be positive or negative: in other words, a person can be motivated to do something, or motivated to avoid doing something. Motivation may also be internally generated (from within the person, e.g. hunger), or externally generated (from the environment, e.g. a social invitation).

The level to which one is motivated will depend on the following factors:

- The desirability of the end goal.
- The ease of achieving the end goal.

One of the problems with studying motivation is that it cannot be inferred from behaviour. For example, a young man may be at a concert in order to hear the music, or he may be there because his girlfriend likes the band and he wanted to give her an enjoyable night out. He may even be there because he plays in a band himself and he wants to see what the competition is doing. His motivation is therefore *subjective* and not available to the observer.

A further complication arises because motivation is rarely simple. Few actions take place as a result of one motivating force; in the example above, several motivations are probably at work, and some of these may not even be apparent to the man in question. It may be that he likes the band, and also wants to impress his girlfriend, but is also avoiding having an evening in with his brother whom he dislikes.

Because motivations may come from many sources, and because it is often impossible to satisfy all one's emotional and physical needs at once, researchers have considered the possibility that needs can be both categorized and prioritized. An early attempt to classify psychological needs was made by Henry Murray, resulting in a list of twenty basic needs. These are: succourance, nurturance, sentience, deference, abasement, defendence, infavoidance, harmavoidance, achievement, counteraction, dominance, aggression, affiliation, autonomy, order, rejection, sex, understanding, exhibition and play.[5]

Virtually all of these needs have marketing implications. The need for rejection is used by Coca-Cola when it urges consumers to reject own-label brands in favour of 'The Real Thing'; the need for nurturance is emphasized in advertisements for cold cures and soups; the need for sentience is appealed to in advertisements for CD-ROM encyclopaedias.

Murray's list is probably not definitive: in other words, there are probably many other needs which are not included in the list. Not all the needs will apply to everybody, and the needs may have differing priorities for different people. Also, some of the needs on the list conflict with each other: for example, dominance and deference. It should also be pointed out that Murray's list was developed as a result of his clinical experience rather than as the result of a research programme, so much of the evidence for the list is anecdotal rather than empirical.

Researchers have therefore tried to establish whether there are certain needs that everyone has in common, and which can be prioritized for most people. The best-known example of this approach is Maslow's hierarchy of need.

Maslow's hierarchy of need

Abraham Maslow[6] hypothesized that needs would be met in a specific order of importance, as shown in Figure 1.2. The theory says that the lower needs will need to be met before the higher needs will assume any importance. For example, somebody marooned on a desert island will (first of all) be concerned with the immediate physiological needs of finding food and water, and perhaps building a shelter. Having met those immediate physiological needs, the next priority might be to ensure that these needs will continue to be met in future: that is, to make the shelter secure against predators, and to gather an emergency supply of food.

Our hypothetical castaway might then want to find other people, a group to belong to; and having found a group, would want to be respected by the group (esteem needs). Having time to think, and to enjoy some kind of artistic endeavour, might come next, followed by a desire to be the best at something, purely for its own sake.

Self-actualization is about achieving self-fulfilment, or one's goal in life. It is the desire to become all that one can be, to achieve everything of which one is capable; sometimes to make a real difference in the world. People operating on the self-actualization level within our own society are usually those who have had a successful career, who have enough financial security to ensure that their physical needs will be met, and who have already won the esteem and respect of their social group. Such people become predominantly interested in the arts, but eventually begin to march to the beat of

Figure 1.2 Maslow's hierarchy of need (Source: Abraham Maslow, Motivation and Personality, New York: Harper and Row, 1954)

their own drums; they will become involved in charity work, or espouse a cause of some sort, or pursue some particularly worthwhile (to them) activity which has no economic return at all.

An example of this is Sir James Goldsmith. A highly successful entrepreneur, he amassed a huge fortune which he then applied (in part) to buying the last remaining Central American rain forest in order to save it from the loggers. Another example is Paul McCartney. Following the break-up of the Beatles, he had two years or so of 'retirement'. As one of the world's richest men, he had no need ever to work again, but he decided that he is, above all, a musician and he formed Wings. The band started out exactly as the Beatles had done, playing in clubs around the country before recording a string of hits.

The hierarchy of need does not necessarily imply that each need must be met before the higher needs can be addressed; merely that the individual's main preoccupation will be with the lower needs until they are met. This means that a tramp may be more interested in spending time with his mates than in finding shelter for the night, or a sales rep may be more interested in winning the sales competition than in earning enough commission to pay the mortgage, but the theory is close enough to the true state of affairs for it to be useful. It should also be noted that circumstances can cause the individual to move down the hierarchy as well as up; the diagram is intended to show the relative importance of each need at a given time, rather than show a life's progression.

Research by McNulty[7] has shown that a greater proportion of the population than ever before are now operating at the self-actualization level of Maslow's hierarchy. These people tend to be individualistic, nonconforming, high-achieving people who commonly are the ones spearheading changes in society. From the viewpoint of the marketer, they are often difficult to deal with, since they do not follow the normal rules. McNulty asserts that these inner-directed people will be in the majority within the next twenty years or so, due to rising wealth and security.

Maslow's hierarchy of need is widely used to explain motivation in such areas as human resource management and sales management. From the viewpoint of consumer behaviour, it may help to explain the rise in independent holidays (at the expense of package tours), the rise in popularity of solo sports such as tennis and skiing (at the expense of team sports such as football and cricket) and the rising interest in experiences such as bungee-jumping (at the expense of the tried-and-tested coach trip to Blackpool).

Certainly it is clear that people in the lowest income brackets are not usually interested in the arts and the aesthetic life, having more important and immediate concerns; but the exceptions (the artist starving in a garret) are so numerous as to call into doubt the universal applicability of the theory.

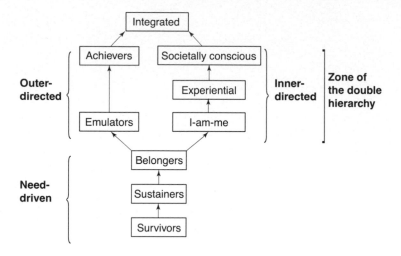

Figure 1.3 Values and lifestyles (Source: Adapted from A. Mitchell, *The Nine American Lifestyles*, New York: Macmillan, 1983)

Maslow's theory adds weight to the development of the VALS structure shown in Figure 1.3 This diagram describes nine different lifestyle options that the researchers at Stanford Research Institute (now SRI International) found in the USA. The same basic lifestyle patterns have also been identified among UK consumers. At the lower levels, which correspond to Maslow's survival, security and belonging needs, the consumers are essentially controlled by their basic needs. After these very basic needs have been met, there is a divergence: some consumers become outer directed, or concerned with the opinions of others, while others become inner directed, concerned with their own internal drives. Ultimately, Mitchell theorizes that consumers adopt an integrated position, where concern and respect for others is combined with a knowledge of their own needs and desires.

A different approach was taken by Fred Herzberg.[8] Herzberg started out as a medical researcher, and became interested in the possibility that some factors might be motivators, whereas others might be demotivators, and the two groups might not necessarily overlap. As a medical man, he called the second group the 'hygiene' factors, since their absence would cause the 'disease' of demotivation.

Fred Herzberg and the hygiene/motivators theory

Herzberg's research was carried out for human resource management purposes, and was intended to give managers an insight into how to motivate their staff to achieve more. He found that factors such as fair pay for the job, reasonable working conditions and a good relationship with the boss were basic to staff contentment, but that more of these things would not motivate staff to perform better. Motivators were found to be such things as the esteem of colleagues, deserved praise from the boss, and promotion.

Translating this into consumer behaviour, some factors in a purchase are basics that every buyer would expect (i.e. the *core benefits* of the product). For example, people expect a car to go from A to B and be reliable. These are hygiene factors, not motivators, since these would be expected by every buyer.

Motivators would tend to be subjective: that is, specific to the individual. Some examples *might* be extra performance, extra comfort, nice styling and so on. In other words, hygiene factors tend to be common to most consumers, whereas motivators are specific to segments and subgroups.

Pain avoidance

Motivation should not be confused with avoidance. Adverse outcomes (pain or other undesirable effects) will not necessarily lead to a positive behavioural activity: in other words, threatening somebody will not necessarily make them do what you want them to do. Despite the frequency of 'cautionary tale' advertising, where the adverse outcomes of not taking a particular course of action are stressed, the motivational effects are uncertain at best.

The reason for this is that rewards can be obtained only by following a specified course of action, whereas there are usually many ways to avoid pain. Burris F. Skinner[9] demonstrated that rats could be taught to push buttons in complex patterns in order to obtain food, and could also learn to avoid electric shocks, but the rats were inventive in the ways they avoided the shocks.

Human beings are, of course, not rats. In this case, though, people are likely to be far more inventive than a rat would be. For example, when the law was passed which made the wearing of seatbelts compulsory, the threat of a £50 fine led to some motorists holding the seatbelt across their chests to avoid being stopped by the police – it did not always result in drivers actually fastening the belts. The result of this, of course, was that drivers were even more likely to have accidents and be injured, since many were driving one-handed.

One way in which marketers can use pain avoidance in motivating consumers is by *modelling*. This is the process whereby consumers are shown the negative consequences of a given action through an actor who

Table 1.3 Using modelling for positive reinforcement

Modelling employed	Desired response
Instructor, expert, salesperson using product (in ads or at point of purchase)	Use product in correct, technically competent way.
Models in ads asking questions at point of purchase	Ask questions at point of purchase that highlight product advantages
Models in ads receiving positive reinforcement for product purchase or use	Try product; increase product purchase and use
Models in ads receiving no reinforcement or receiving punishment for performing undesired behaviours	Extinction or decrease of undesired behaviours
Individual or group (similar to target) using product in novel, enjoyable way	Use product in new ways

Source: Walter R. Nord and J. Paul Peter, 'A behaviour modification perspective on marketing', *Journal of Marketing*, vol. 44 (Spring 1980), pp. 36–47.

acts as a model. For example, an advertisement might show a commuter who has been prosecuted for fare dodging, complete with a detailed account of the consequences of the action ('It was the embarrassment of having to stand up in court and admit fiddling a £1.30 fare. And I lost my job.'). Another example might be a housewife whose washing powder 'Can't shift those greasy stains'. In each case, the consumer is invited to see the possible negative consequences of fiddling the fare, or using the wrong washing powder.

Modelling can also be used for positive reinforcement, of course. Further examples are given in Table 1.3.

Hedonism

Hedonism is the cult of pleasure. In terms of consumer behaviour, it concerns those areas which attach to the fun of owning something. For example, car manufacturers design car doors to close with a satisfying 'thunk'. This serves no useful purpose except to make the driver and passengers feel that they are in a solid, secure vehicle. Likewise great care was taken with the design of the Ford Transit van to ensure comfort for the driver. This was because many Transits are owner operated, and comfort is an issue.

Further examples abound. The foil seals on jars of coffee are pleasurable to pop; the turquoise colour of the Heinz Beans label enhances the orange colour of the beans so that they look more appetising when opened; Apple Mac software includes cartoon images to make work more fun (e.g. eyeballs which watch the cursor moving). In some cases these hedonic aspects have come about almost by accident, as a by-product of the packaging design; in other cases the hedonic attributes of the product are deliberately added at the design stage.

Not surprisingly, these aspects of products encourage people to buy them. Being human is much more about having fun and enjoying things than it is about mere survival; as a species, most of us have already solved most of the problems of day-to-day survival. People are therefore prepared to pay a small premium in order to have products that are fun to own and use, or which increase the pleasure of living. This is particularly true in western industrialized countries, and even more so among wealthy individuals.

In terms of advertising, many adverts use hedonic images to promote products. Cadbury's Flake shows a woman losing herself in the pleasure of eating the chocolate; the recent series of Rover advertisements emphasize the comfort of the car by comparing it with a womb environment; and even the Boddington's beer adverts (the cream of Manchester) emphasize the luxurious nature of the product, albeit in a humorous way.

Hedonic approaches to the design and promotion of products abound because consumers can generally obtain the core benefits of the products from any of the brands on offer. The marketer can often best differentiate the brand by offering the consumer a little extra fun or pleasure from using the product.

Key points from this chapter

In this chapter we have looked at what motivates people to buy. In particular, we have looked at drives, needs, wants and motives, and the hedonic aspects of purchase behaviour. Below are the key points made.

- Many motives are irrational or unconscious.
- Need is a perceived lack; want is a specific satisfier.
- Drive is caused by the gap between desired and actual states.
- Most marketing is about activating needs and directing wants.
- Motivation is complex and cannot be inferred from behaviour.
- Needs can be ranked, but there is considerable overlap.
- As wealth increases, motivation changes.
- Many, even most, purchases are motivated in part by hedonic goals.

Notes

1. Morris P. Holbrook and Elizabeth C. Hirschmann, 'The experiential aspects of consumption: consumer fantasies, feelings and fun', *Journal of Consumer Research*, vol. 9 (September 1982), pp. 132–40.
2. Melvin Copeland, *Principles of Merchandising'* (Chicago, IL: A.W. Shaw, 1924).
3. James F. Engel, Roger D. Blackwell, and Paul W. Miniard, *Consumer Behaviour*, 8th edn (Fort Worth, TX: Dryden Press, 1995).
4. P.S. Raju, 'Optimum stimulation level: its relationship to personality, demographics and exploratory behaviour', *Journal of Consumer Research*, vol. 7 (December 1980), pp. 272–82.
5. Henry A. Murray, *An Exploration in Personality: A clinical experimental study of fifty men of college age* (London: Oxford University Press, 1938).
6. Abraham Maslow, *Motivation and Personality* (New York: Harper and Row, 1954).
7. W. Kirk McNulty, 'UK social change through a wide-angle lens', *Futures*, August 1985.
8. F. Herzberg, *Work and the Nature of Man* (London: Collins, 1966).
9. Burris F. Skinner, *Science and Human Behaviour* (New York: Macmillan, 1953).

2

Goals and incentives, uncertainty and post-purchase dissonance

---

This chapter is about the things that people strive for, and the aftermath of achieving those aims. After reading the chapter, you should be able to:

- Explain how goals are arrived at.
- Describe different types of goal.
- Show how consumers can minimize uncertainty.
- Develop methods for minimizing post-purchase dissonance.

Goals

A goal is an external object towards which a motive is directed.[1] Goals differ from drives in that the goal is external, and pulls the person in a given direction; a drive is internal and pushes the individual.

In this way, a goal acts as an incentive to take a course of action (or refrain from taking action, as the case may be). When an individual has a drive which needs to be addressed, there may be a series of goals which would satisfy the drive. For example, someone may be feeling bored and in need of entertainment. This leads to a drive to find something to do, which leads to a possible goal choice, as shown in Table 2.1. The basic goal of being entertained can be met in many different ways, and marketers do well to remember that consumers always have a choice.

The basic consequences, needs or values that consumers want to achieve are called *end goals*. These end goals can be *concrete* or *abstract*. Concrete end goals derive directly from the product purchase, whereas abstract end goals derive indirectly from the purchase.

Table 2.1 Examples of possible goal choices

Goal	Possible subgoals	Action
Go to the cinema	Choose a film	Look in the evening paper, make a choice
Visit friends	Decide which friends to see	Phone around to see who's at home
Watch TV	Which channel?	Look in the TV guide
Rent a video	Which video?	Visit the video rental shop
Read a book	Which book?	Choose one from the shelves

Below are some examples of each type of end goal.

- Concrete end goals: Going to buy a light-bulb. Although the purpose of buying the light-bulb is to replace a broken one, the bulb itself is the direct reason for the journey.

  Buying a sandwich. The purpose of the purchase is to satisfy the hunger by eating the sandwich. The goal derives directly from the purchase.

  Buying a car because you get a job that is a long way away. The end goal here is the need for transportation, a concrete goal.

- Abstract end goals: Buying a bottle of wine so you can go to a party. The party is the end goal, not drinking the wine (which is probably why so much cheap wine arrives at parties).

  Buying some new clothes to go to an interview. The job is the end goal; the clothes are only a means to the end.

  Buying a posh car to impress the neighbours. The end goal is impressing the neighbours.

In both cases the end goals could be met by some other means: in the first instance, lighting a candle would also provide light if there were no light-bulbs available. Equally, chips or a pizza might be equally acceptable instead of the sandwich, or buying a railway season ticket might work out cheaper than a car.

Abstract end goals can usually be met with a much broader range of possibilities. You could go to the party with a friend who already has a bottle, or you could take food instead, or you could even sneak in without bringing anything – though this will not make you popular! Likewise you could borrow some smart clothes, or go in what you have and trust to your brilliance to get you the job. Neighbours could be equally impressed if you had a swimming-pool installed, or went on an expensive holiday.

Abstract goals are usually intangible, and often relate to hedonic or irrational motives, but this is not always the case as the job interview example shows.

Problems with goals

Some end goals are too general for the consumer to be able to make any real judgements based on them. For example, a person who says, 'I just want to be happy' may not have any idea of how to achieve this. On a more concrete level, saying 'I want to buy a decent computer' is not much help to the salesperson who is trying to find a machine that will meet the customer's needs. In this case, the customer clearly does not know enough about the technicalities to be able to make a reasonable decision alone. 'I want to be respected' is equally a goal which is difficult to develop a strategy for.

Table 2.2 gives some purchase end goals and motivations, with examples. In practice, marketers have little influence over consumers' main goals, since these often derive from basic values. Marketers can try to

Table 2.2 Examples of purchase end goals

Dominant end goal	Basic purchase motivation	Examples
Optimize satisfaction	Seek maximum positive consequences	Buy dinner at the best restaurant in town, rather than risking a cheap diner
Prevention	Avoid potential unpleasant consequences	Buy rustproofing for a new car so as to maintain the good appearance of the car, and its trade-in value
Resolve conflict	Seek satisfactory balance of positive and negative consequences	Buy a moderately expensive car of very good quality so as to avoid high maintenance costs and unreliability, while still keeping within a reasonable expenditure
Escape	Reduce or escape from current aversive circumstances	Buy a shampoo to get rid of dandruff, and so avoid embarrassment
Maintenance (satisfice)	Maintain satisfaction of basic need with minimal effort	Buy bread at the local corner shop. This satisfies the need for bread without having to go to the out-of-town hypermarket where you do your main weekly shopping.

influence the less abstract end goals, such as the desired functional or psychosocial consequences, through promotional strategies.

For instance, although it is difficult to persuade somebody that he or she ought to dress to impress, we can influence those who already want to dress to impress that they should buy our clothes. Examples of this abound, as the following list shows:

- *If you want to get ahead, get a hat*. This was a slogan thought of during the 1950s when the wearing of hats was going out of fashion. In fact the slogan was not very successful; hats still went out of fashion, and have only returned to the fashion scene in the 1980s and 1990s.
- *Man at C&A*. The impression from this series of 1970s advertisements was that men could buy smart casual clothes at reasonable prices from the C&A chain. Men were already buying casual clothes; the main goal was therefore already in place.
- *Any Levi's ad*. Advertisements for Levi's jeans are aimed at young people looking for smart casual wear, and are not particularly intended to encourage people to wear jeans. The intention is to encourage people who intend to buy a new pair of jeans to buy Levi's rather than Wranglers.

None of the above examples seeks to persuade people to buy clothes; all of them seek to persuade people to buy *specific* clothes. In other words, the basic goal is left untouched, but the end goals are presented in a desirable way.

It is not always feasible for an individual to go straight for an end goal. In fact, it is far more common for consumers to establish a series of subsidiary goals which will lead, eventually, to the end goal.

Goal hierarchies are series of subgoals that provide a structure for decision making: in other words, people set priorities. If the individual has previous experience, this will help; consumers without previous experience will have more trouble with establishing goal hierarchies and are likely to go by trial and error. For example, if you have never bought a car before, you do not really know what to look for; you will not have prioritized your needs, or formed a hierarchy of goals. Below is a sample goal hierarchy for buying a second-hand car.

1. Find out which car would best suit your needs.
2. Find out which is the cheapest way of financing the purchase.
3. Find out who has the right type of car for you.
4. Do the deal and get the car.

To translate this into an action plan, the person will have to establish a series of activities to meet each subgoal. Here is an example of the buying process for the second-hand car:

1. Buy used-car guide, *What Car?* or equivalent.
2. Decide which looks like the make(s) and year(s) that most suit your needs.
3. Decide what prices are within your range.
4. Phone around loan companies to get the best loan quotes.
5. Buy the local paper as soon as it hits the newsagents.
6. Call up anybody who seems to have the right kind of car, call round to see it, and do the deal.

The experienced consumer – for example, somebody who often buys second-hand cars – will already know how to go about this process and will establish the goal hierarchy and action plan immediately. Inexperienced consumers have to construct a goal hierarchy from scratch, often by trial-and-error approaches, and develop a decision plan to achieve each subgoal. Marketers can help here, and especially salespeople, because they can guide individuals through the process; this is the most effective kind of selling activity, since it addresses the consumer's need for assistance.

Problem-solving processes are greatly affected by the amount of product knowledge the consumer has acquired through past experiences, and by the level of involvement with the product and/or choice processes. In other words, if the individual has a great deal of knowledge about the product category, or has a strong interest in the product category, the process of finding a suitable product will proceed along very different lines. The inexperienced car buyer is more likely to follow a plan such as this:

1. Decide to buy a car.
2. Ask around among family and friends to find out which car might suit his or her needs. This would often involve a discussion to determine what the needs are; an experienced car-owner might suggest extra needs which the prospective purchaser is not aware of. The financing of the purchase might be discussed at this point.
3. Go to used-car showrooms to examine the different makes and models.
4. Find a helpful salesperson who appears honest and trustworthy.
5. Tell the salesperson what the needs are.
6. Listen to the salesperson's advice about the particular models in stock. Again, the financing of the purchase might also be discussed at this stage.
7. Make the decision based on the closeness of fit between the salesperson's description of the car and the needs that have been identified.
8. Buy the car.

For example, compare the purchasing behaviour of a camera buff with that of a 'snapshot' photographer. The camera buff will know which type of lens is best, which camera bodies are most reliable and durable, and which accessories (light meters, etc.) will give the best results. A camera buff will use different filters for different effects, and so forth. This type of consumer will probably shop at a specialist camera shop, and will talk on equal terms with the sales staff.

The snapshot enthusiast, on the other hand, is likely to want a camera that is simple and relatively foolproof, and that will give reliable if uninspiring results. This individual will probably shop at Boots or Dixons and will not be very interested in the technicalities of shutter speeds, apertures or film speeds.

Risk and uncertainty

In the case of the inexperienced buyer, there is a greater risk attached to making the purchase. Inexperienced buyers have, by definition, less knowledge of the product category they are planning to buy into. Most consumers will try to reduce risk in this situation, and indeed this is part of the reason for establishing goal hierarchies; the task is thus broken down into manageable portions which can each take a share of the risk. The risks fall into the categories shown in Table 2.3.

The amount of perceived risk a consumer experiences depends on two factors: first, how serious the downside is, or in other words whether the possible negative consequences of the purchase will have a serious effect; second, the probability that the negative consequences will occur. This means that somebody considering the risk of buying a new climbing rope will be aware that the possible consequence of the rope breaking will be death or serious injury. The experienced climber will know which type of

Table 2.3 Types of purchasing risk

Type of risk	Explanation	Examples
Physical risk	The fear of injury from the product	Buying a car with defective brakes; buying a cold remedy with unpleasant side-effects
Financial risk	Losing or wasting money	Buying a car that depreciates quickly; buying a computer and finding that the price has fallen to half within three months
Functional risk	Finding out that the product will not do the job you bought it for	Buying a car that breaks down constantly; buying a painkiller that does not stop the pain
Psychosocial risk	The fear of looking foolish	Buying a suit that your friends think looks weird on you; buying a car with a poor reputation

rope to buy to minimize the risk of breakage. Consumers habitually reduce risk in this way. Conversely, if a consumer is thinking of trying a new brand of biscuits, the possible downside is only financial, and is probably less than a pound; even if the biscuits taste terrible, the risk is small so a trial purchase is more likely.

The main way in which consumers reduce risk in purchasing is by increasing their knowledge about the product category. If the risk is still perceived as being high, the consumer will simply not make the purchase. For this reason marketers, particularly retailers, seek to reduce the perceived risk in the consumers' mind by offering no-quibble return policies. A recent example of this is the Tesco's return policy, under which even partly consumed or perishable products can be returned for refund or replacement without any questions or arguments.

Consumers will often spend a great deal of time and effort shopping around, acquiring the necessary knowledge to reduce risk. This has been compared to the hunter-gatherer behaviour of our ancestors, and may account for the fact that the vast majority of retail purchases are still made in High Street stores rather than through catalogues or mail order.

Heuristics

In order to reduce risk, and to simplify the decision-making process, consumers will usually have a set of *heuristics*. These are simple 'if . . . then' decision-making rules which can be established before the search procedure begins. Heuristics are also subject to alteration in the light of new knowledge, so some may be constructed as the search procedure continues. Heuristics can be divided into three categories: *search heuristics*, which are concerned with rules for finding out information; *evaluation heuristics*, which are concerned with rules for judging products; and *choice heuristics*, which are procedures for comparing evaluations of alternatives. Some examples are given in Table 2.4.

Heuristics can be used by the consumer to simplify decision making. They may be stored in the consumer's memory, or may be constructed on the spot based on information received, but either way they allow the consumer to reach rapid decisions without overstretching his or her *cognitive capacity* or brainpower.

The use of heuristics, in the extreme, leads to habitual behaviour. For example, there are people who will go to the same pub every Friday night and order the same drinks and sit at the same table as they always use. *Routinized choice behaviour* such as this is comforting and relaxing, since it does not involve any real decision making at all. In most cases, though,

Table 2.4 Examples of heuristics

Search heuristics	Examples
Store selection	If you are buying stereo equipment, go to Sam's Hi-Fi.
Sources of information	If you want to know which alternatives are worth searching for, read the test reports in *Which?*
Source credibility	If a magazine accepts advertisements from the tested products, do not believe its product tests.
Evaluation heuristics	**Examples**
Key criteria	If comparing processed foods, examine sugar content.
Negative criteria	If a salient consequence is negative (high sugar content), give this choice criterion extra weight in the integration process.
Significant differences	If the alternatives are similar on a salient consequence (all low sugar), ignore that choice criterion.
Choice heuristics	**Examples**
For familiar, frequently purchased products	*If choosing among familiar products . . .*
Works best	Choose the product that you think works best – that provides the best level of performance on the most relevant functional consequences.
Affect referral	Choose the alternative you like best (select the alternative with the most favourable attitude).
Bought last	Select the alternative you used last, if it was satisfactory.
Important person	Choose the alternative that some 'important person' (spouse, child, friend) likes.
Price-based rule	Buy the least expensive alternative (or buy the most expensive, depending on your beliefs about the relationship of price to product quality).
Promotion rule	Choose an alternative for which you have a coupon or that you can get at a price reduction (seasonal sale, promotional rebate, special price reduction).
For new, unfamiliar products	*If choosing among unfamiliar products . . .*
Wait and see	Don't buy any software until someone you know has used it for at least a month and recommends it. Don't buy a new car (computer, etc.) until the second model year.
Expert consultant	Find an expert or more knowledgeable person, have them evaluate the alternatives in terms of your goals, then buy the alternative that the expert selects.

Source: Adapted from Wayne D. Hoyer,
'An examination of consumer decision making for a common repeat purchase product',
Journal of Consumer Research, vol. 10 (December 1984), pp. 822–9.

heuristics are simple decision rules (for example, 'When choosing a restaurant in a foreign country, always eat where the locals eat').

Interrupts

Interrupts are events which prevent the consumer from following the goal hierarchy. There are four types:

- *Unexpected information, inconsistent with established beliefs.* For example, if the shop which the consumer had expected to buy from has changed hands or closed, the consumer has to rearrange the goals to encompass finding a new supplier.
- *Prominent environmental stimuli*: for example, an in-store display showing a new brand at a big discount. This may divert the consumer away from his or her normal brand choice, or at the very least cause the consumer to consider the possibility of switching.
- *Affective states.* Hunger, boredom or tiredness during a shopping trip may lead to a change in the goal. This may be a change away from looking for a new outfit, and towards a search for a cup of tea and a sit-down.
- *Conflicts.* These are of three types. First, there are *approach–approach conflicts*, where two different products offer the same (or similar) benefit. A holiday in Greece or a holiday in Spain may seem equally attractive, so the consumer is drawn equally to each one. Second, there are *avoidance–avoidance conflicts*. A consumer may not want to be embarrassed by wearing old shoes, but equally may not want to spend money on new ones. Third, there are *approach–avoidance* conflicts. In this case there are factors in favour of the purchase, but also factors against: for example, a stereo may be on special offer, but the consumer does not know if the quality is good. The consumer is therefore torn between wanting to buy at a cheaper price, and being afraid of a functional risk of buying a product that doesn't do what it is supposed to do.

The effect of interrupts will depend on how consumers interpret the interrupting event. On the one hand, the interrupt may activate new end goals (as when a long shopping trip dissolves into a search for a cup of tea). On the other hand, a *choice heuristic* may be activated (for example, if a friend recommends a brand). Sometimes the problem-solving behaviour might be blocked or shelved indefinitely (say by loss of job).

The strength of the interrupt is important. Is the hunger severe enough to stop you shopping for things you need for tonight? Can you skip lunch for once?

In most cases, consumers tend to resume an interrupted problem-solving task. This means that, although a marketer might be able to distract shoppers from their appointed tasks long enough to buy a cup of coffee or watch a demonstration, the shoppers will return to what they were doing afterwards. It is, in other words, difficult to dissuade consumers from following their goal hierarchies.

Post-purchase dissonance

Post-purchase dissonance occurs when the purchase turns out to be not quite what was expected. It can come about through misunderstanding, mistake or deception, or sometimes through plain old second thoughts or new information arising.

The mechanism by which it arises is simple. When working through the goal hierarchy, the consumer will form a view of what it will be like to own the product, and will develop a *perceptual map* of the anticipated benefits. This is a mental picture of what life will be like with the product included. Richard Oliver's expectancy disconfirmation model says that satisfaction or dissatisfaction is the result of comparing pre-purchase expectations and post-purchase outcomes.[2]

These pre-purchase expectations fall into three categories: *equitable performance,*[3] which is a judgement regarding the performance one could reasonably expect given the cost and effort of obtaining the product; *ideal performance,*[4] which is what the consumer really hoped the product would do; and *expected performance,*[5] which is what the product probably will do. If later experience shows that the product has different attributes, and the expected benefits do not materialize, the consumer feels a discord (or dissonance) since there is a clash between anticipation and actuality.

The level of dissonance will depend on the following factors:

- The degree of divergence between the expected outcome and the actual outcome.
- The importance of the discrepancy to the individual.
- The degree to which the discrepancy can be corrected.
- The cost of purchase (in terms of time and money).

For example, if a consumer buys a stereo player which turns out to have a scratch on the lid, this is probably only a minor fault that is easily corrected. Therefore the dissonance will not be great. In some cases, the consumer may even accept the scratch without seeking redress from the supplier; if the scratch is a small one, it probably just is not worth pursuing. Some research[6] has shown that only one-third of consumers will complain or seek redress; the remainder will boycott the products in future, or simply complain to others. In the case of minor dissonance, or high cost of complaint (for instance, returning products to a duty-free shop in Istanbul Airport) this is perfectly understandable.

Conversely, if the stereo has poor quality sound reproduction, this could be a major discrepancy between the expected outcome (good sound) and the actual outcome (poor sound). It is also unlikely that the hi-fi shop will exchange the product, since there is not necessarily an actual malfunction; merely poor performance. In this case, the dissonance will be great.

From a marketer's viewpoint, it is important to reduce post-purchase dissonance. The evidence is that consumers will try to do so themselves, often by complaining about the product. If they do not get any redress from the supplier, they will complain about the product to their friends and family. There are four general approaches that consumers take to reducing dissonance, as follows:

- Ignore the dissonant information and look for positive (consonant) information about the product. (For example, the car may be slower than you expected, but it's built like a tank!)
- Distort the dissonant information. (Sure it's slow, but compared with what? It's faster than a Ford Escort).
- Play down the importance of the issue. (So it's slow. I still get there, don't I?)
- Change one's behaviour. (Trade it in. Get something else. Go by bicycle.)

Marketers are able to 'plug into' these approaches. Some car manufacturers, aware that their cars are reliable rather than exciting, will use this in their advertising. For example, Volkswagen ran a recent advertising campaign with the slogan, 'If only everything in life was as reliable as a Volkswagen.' In general, it is better to avoid the occurrence of post-purchase dissonance by ensuring that the consumer has accurate information about the product and its performance: in other words, ensuring that the consumer's perceptual map of the product conforms as closely as possible with later experience of using the product.

If post-purchase dissonance does occur, the consumer may take action against the producer to redress the situation. For this reason it would be careless to assume that the marketing job has finished once the sale is completed. The consumer's actions tend to fall into one of the following three general categories: *voice responses*, where the customer comes back to the producer to complain or seek a refund; *private responses*, where the customer generates negative word-of-mouth by complaining to family and friends; and *third-party responses*, where the customer takes legal action or complains to a consumer rights organization.[7]

When faced with *voice responses*, managers and consumers may not agree on the legitimacy of the complaint. Managers will sometimes feel that the consumer wants something for nothing, or may even feel that there is an implied personal criticism in the complaint. Consumers will always feel that there should be some response to the complaint, and the way in which the complaint is handled affects satisfaction and dissatisfaction.[8] One study has shown that, as the level of complaints increases, the willingness of managers to listen decreases.[9] This naturally tends to lead to an increase in the number of complaints, since managers are less likely to put right whatever is going wrong, and a vicious circle develops.

Third-party responses can range from a complaint to the Trading Standards Officer through to legal action. In virtually all such cases, the consumer will already have given a voice response; if not, the Trading Standards Officer or solicitor will urge the consumer to do so before further action is taken. Clearly a legal case is unlikely to be successful if the supplier has not been given the chance to put matters right. In the event that a complaint does end up with a lawyer or consumer organization, it is usually better to try to be co-operative with the third party rather than be obstructive. For example, using a blanket 'no comment' statement to a consumer affairs reporter is likely to look very much like an admission of guilt.

The following factors appear to affect whether or not a complaint will be made:[10]

- The significance of the consumption event in terms of product import-ance, cost, social visibility and time required in consumption. Consumers will be unlikely to complain if the product is cheap and unimportant, and was not expected to last long anyway.

- The consumer's knowledge and experience: the number of previous purchases, level of product knowledge, perception of ability as a con-sumer, and previous complaining experience. Consumers who have frequently complained in the past are more likely to do so in future; consumers with substantial knowledge of the product category are more likely to complain if things go wrong.

- The difficulty of seeking redress, in terms of time, cost and nuisance. Consumers are unlikely to complain if the product was purchased some way away, or if complaining would involve a disproportionate amount of time and trouble.

- The perceived probability that a complaint will lead to a positive outcome.[11] Complaints are more likely if the consumer has a guarantee, or feels that he or she is dealing with a reputable firm which will resolve the problem. Also, consumers are less likely to complain if the problem is perceived as being incapable of being put right or compensated for.

Since there is ample evidence to show that putting a complaint right actually increases the likelihood of the customer remaining loyal to the producer, and consequently purchasing in future, it would seem sensible to encourage customers to voice their complaints rather than use *private responses* or (worse still) *third-party responses*.[12]

Key points from this chapter

In this chapter we have looked at goals, post-purchase dissonance and risk. Consumers make purchases in order to achieve goals. These may not be the most obvious ones, since most goals are subjective. Here are the main points from the chapter:

- Drive is internal and pushes the individual.
- A goal is an external object to which a motive is directed; goals pull the individual.
- Goals can be concrete or abstract.
- There may be a hierarchy of goals – subgoals that have to be achieved before the main goal can be met.
- Most marketing activities are likely to be aimed at the subgoals rather than the main goals.
- Interrupts may activate new end goals, but most consumers will revert to the original end goal following an interrupt.
- Many marketing activities are designed to interrupt the goal-satisfying process.
- Risks can be physical, financial, functional or psychosocial.
- Post-purchase, the consumer may re-evaluate the product in terms of whether it has achieved the goals – if it fails, this leads to post-purchase dissonance.
- Post-purchase dissonance occurs when anticipation exceeds actuality.
- Consumers may not always voice their complaints to the supplier, but it is in the supplier's best interests to encourage them to do so.

Notes

1. Sak Onkvisit and John J. Shaw, *Consumer Behaviour, Strategy and Analysis* (New York: Macmillan, 1994).

2. Richard L. Oliver, 'A cognitive model of the antecedents and consequences of satisfaction decisions', *Journal of Marketing Research*, vol. 17 (November 1980), pp. 460–9).

3. Robert B. Woodruff, Ernst R. Cadotte and Roger L. Jenkins, 'Modelling consumer satisfaction using experienced-based norms', *Journal of Marketing Research*, vol. 20 (August 1983), pp. 296–304.

4. Morris B. Holbrook, 'Situation-specific ideal points and usage of multiple dissimilar brands', in Jagdesh N. Sheth (ed.), *Research in Marketing*, vol. 7 (Greenwich, CT: JAI Press, 1984).

5. M. Leichty and Gilbert A. Churchill, Jr, 'Conceptual insights into consumer satisfaction and services', in Neil Beckwith *et al.*, (eds.), *Educators Conference Proceedings* (Chicago, IL: American Marketing Association, 1979).

6. Ralph L. Day, Klaus Brabicke, Thomas Schaetzle, and Fritz Staubach, 'The hidden agenda of consumer complaining', *Journal of Retailing*, vol. 57 (Fall 1981), pp. 86–106.

7. Kathy J. Cobb, Gary C. Walgren and Mary Hollowed, 'Differences in organisational responses to consumer letters of satisfaction and dissatisfaction', in Melanie Wallendorf and Paul Anderson (eds.), *Advances in Consumer Research*, vol. 14 (Provo, UT: Association for Consumer Research, 1987).

8. *Ibid.*

9. Denise T. Smart and Charles L. Martin, 'Manufacturer responsiveness to consumer correspondence: an empirical investigation of consumer perceptions', *Journal of Consumer Affairs*, vol. 26 (Summer 1991), pp. 104–28.

10. Ralph L. Day, 'Modelling choices among alternative responses to dissatisfaction', in Thomas C. Kinnear (ed.), *Advances in Consumer Research*, vol. 11 (Provo, UT: Association for Consumer Research, 1984).

11. Diane Halstead and Cornelia Droge, 'Consumer attitudes towards complaining and the prediction of multiple complaint responses' in R. Holman and M. Solomon, *Advances in Consumer Research*, vol. 18 (Provo, UT: Association for Consumer Research, 1991).

12. Christopher Power, 'How to get closer to your customers', *Business Week* (Enterprise 1993 edition), p. 44.

3

Personality, traits, self-concept, routines and habits

This chapter is about some of the factors which make up the individual person. After reading this chapter, you should be able to:

- Explain Goffman's life-as-theatre analogy.
- Describe the problems of studying personality.
- Describe the features of personality, and some of its dimensions.
- Describe and compare the four main approaches to the study of personality.
- Explain how self-concept affects purchasing behaviour.
- Link theories of personality to examples of consumer behaviour.

Roles, and life as theatre

People create and project images of themselves to other people; these images are called *roles*. The role may change according to the circumstances and environment which the individual is in: for example, a person's behaviour in church is different from the same person's behaviour in a disco or a pub, and equally people behave differently with friends from the way they behave when with their parents or family.

This role-playing behaviour is natural, and not consciously carried out; people do not consciously change their accents, movements and statements to fit in with the people around them. Nevertheless, most people do end up acting in ways which will be acceptable to those around them, and by doing so are conferred a status within the group. In most cases, this status is merely that of being accepted within the group (which, of course, helps to

Table 3.1 Examples of life as theatre

Theatrical terms	Explanation	Real-life example
Props	Items used to make gestures, or to support and emphasize movement, or to set a scene	Cigarettes, walking-sticks, furniture and ornaments
Costume	Items of clothing which serve to establish a role, or set a scene	Sportswear, business suits, power dressing
Stage	The place where the performance is held, and where the audience is assembled	Offices, living-rooms, pubs, churches
Backstage	The place where the dressing-rooms are; where the actors prepare for the performance, and where they meet their friends and intimates	Where the individual lives or is relaxed; home; where the person's friends and intimates can visit
Make-up	The face the actor puts on to emphasize the characterization	Cosmetics, perfumes, aftershave, hairdressing
Script	A pre-planned set of statements intended to communicate the role to the audience	Jokes, sayings, conversational styles, professional jargon
Business	The movements actors make in the course of playing the role	Gestures, body language, facial expressions used to convey emotions and ideas
Applause	Feedback from the audience; confirmation that the role projection has been effective	Getting your way in a business negotiation, having friends laugh at your jokes, having a conversational response from a friend

fulfil the person's need to belong), but most people would prefer it if they were openly welcomed into the group, and given a degree of respect; this would fulfil the person's esteem needs.

Erving Goffman[1] developed a useful analogy for the role-playing behaviour when he developed his life-as-theatre analogy. According to Goffman, everyday life has much in common with theatre: people use script, props, make-up, costume and movement to convey an image of themselves to the 'audience'. For Goffman, there is even a backstage – we have friends, lovers or spouses who are allowed 'in the dressing room' to see us as we really are, relaxed and with all the props put away and the make-up off. Table 3.1 shows some examples of Goffman's analogy.

It is important to understand that the role playing described here is not in any way a false or 'two-faced' activity. Everybody plays different roles according to circumstances and environment; only to those with whom we are backstage do we show our true faces, and even then there is often some play acting going on, for the purpose of enhancing our own image or getting our own way. Goffman himself is careful to point out that the analogy should not be pushed too far; we should be aware that the role playing described by Goffman is actually part of the real everyday lives of real people, not the contrived parts played by actors.

Personality

Personality is the collection of individual characteristics that make a person unique, and which control an individual's responses to and relationship with the external environment. It is a composite of subordinate processes: for example, attitude, motivation and perception. It is the whole of the person, and is the system that governs behaviour rather than the behaviour itself.

The elements that make up personality are called *traits*. Considerable research effort has been made to link individual personality traits to buying behaviour, but with limited success. This is despite the apparent logic that people would buy products that reflect their personality traits (for example, outgoing flamboyant people might be expected to buy more colourful clothing). In fact, there is some evidence that personality relates to new product purchasing behaviour, and there is more on this in a later chapter; there is also some evidence that inner and outer directedness affect some buying behaviour (see Chapter 2). Overall, though, it is the total personality that dictates buying behaviour rather than each individual trait.

Personality has the following features:

- It is *integrated*: that is to say, all the factors making up the personality act on each other to produce an integrated whole.

- It is *self-serving*. The characteristics of personality facilitate the attainment of needs and goals. In other words, the personality exists to meet its own needs.

- Personal characteristics are *individualistic* and unique, in degree and intensity as well as presence. Although many personal characteristics are shared with other people, the possible number of combinations of traits is huge, and therefore each individual is different. This is what makes each person a separate and unique being.

- Personality is *overt*. External behaviour is affected by personality. In other words, the personality can be observed (albeit indirectly) and deduced from the person's behaviour.

- Personality is *consistent*. Once a person's basic personality has been established, it will change only slowly and with some difficulty; for practical purposes, an individual consumer's personality will stay constant throughout the buying process.

Because people are individuals, it is difficult for marketers to take a standardized approach, yet the exigencies of the business world require standardization. For this reason, many attempts have been made to establish groupings of personality types which can be approached with a standardized offering. This is one of the bases of segmentation (the process of dividing the market into target groups of customers with similar needs). For this reason, and of course for the purposes of treating abnormal personalities, there is a long history of studying personality.

Approaches to studying personality

There are four basic approaches:

- The *psychoanalytic* approach. Here the emphasis is on psychoanalysis, or studying the processes and events which have led to the development of personality traits. The focus is on the individual. This approach is typified by Freudianism.
- *Typology.* Here the individuals are grouped according to recognized types.
- *Trait and factor theories.* Here the individual traits of the personality are examined as factors making up the whole.
- *Psychographics.* The consumers are measured using their behavioural tendencies in order to infer personality traits.

These four basic approaches deserve a more comprehensive explanation.

The Freudian approach is very much centred on the individual. Here the researcher (or, more usually, psychologist) asks the patient or subject to talk about anything regardless of logic, courtesy, self-defence, etc. A Freudian would analyze these statements in terms of id, ego and superego.

According to Freud, the *id* is the underlying drive of the psyche. It is the source of the most basic, instinctive forces that cause people to behave in particular ways, and is largely operating below the conscious level. The *ego* is the conscious self, the part of the mind that makes the day-to-day decisions which lead to the satisfaction of the id; the *superego* is an internalized parent, the conscience that holds us back from selfish gratification of the id's needs. The superego is also operating mostly below the conscious level, and is the 'brake' on behaviour; in a sense, the ego is constantly making compromises between the id's demands and the superego's restraints. This is illustrated in Figure 3.1.

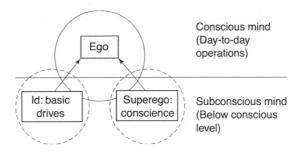

Figure 3.1 Freudian model of the mind

In simple terms, the id acts like a spoilt child, demanding instant gratification regardless of consequences; the superego acts like a stern parent, urging self-restraint and devotion to duty; and the ego acts like a good lawyer, arranging compromises and settlements between the two parties which will not lead to bankruptcy.

The Freudian approach led to motivation research, which purported to explain the underlying reasons for buying. Motivation research was at its most popular in the 1950s and was, for a time, believed to be able to predict consumer behaviour in terms of basic drives which supposedly came from the id. Some of the claims made for motivational research now seem wild or ridiculous: for example, it was claimed that crunching cornflakes appealed to the killer instinct because it sounds like crunching animal bones, and that baking a cake is a substitute for giving birth. Convertible cars were thought to be a substitute for a girlfriend, and so forth. Motivational research became somewhat discredited because of the extravagant claims made, but it still has something to say to marketers.

The *depth* (or *guided*) *interview* is an example of motivational research methodology which is still widely used. A small number of respondents (50 or fewer) is interviewed without the use of a formal list of questions. Interviewees are encouraged to express their innermost thoughts and feelings about the object of the research (perhaps a new product). The interviewer needs considerable skill to keep the interview on course without leading the interviewee.

A variation on this is the *focus group,* in which a group of ten or so respondents is invited to discuss their feelings and motivations collectively. The advantage of this method is that the respondents will tend to stimulate each other, and therefore there is less risk of the interviewer introducing bias into the results.

Projective tests are widely used in psychological counselling and psychiatry, and occasionally have applications in market research. They are based on the assumption that the individual may sometimes have difficulty in answering questions directly, either because the answers would be embarrassing or because the answers do not readily come to mind. In effect, a projective technique requires the respondent to say what somebody else might think about a given topic. Sometimes this is done by showing the respondent a cartoon strip of people in a relevant situation; sometimes the respondent is asked to complete a sentence; sometimes the respondent will be asked to draw a picture describing his or her feelings about the attitudinal object. In all cases the intention of the research is to allow the respondents to convey their innermost feelings in a non-personal way.

Motivational researchers tend to be interested in the id, claiming that this dictates the individual's basic drives. The assumption is that knowledge of the id's demands will enable the marketers to shape arguments for the ego to use in overcoming the superego's restraining influence.

Hedonic consumption

Hedonic consumption appeals to the id. It is defined as 'those facets of consumer behaviour that relate to the multisensory, fantasy and emotive aspects of one's experience with products'.[2] Hedonism is about satisfying the 'animal' needs of the individual. An example of this is the recent billboard advertisements for Club 18–30 holidays, using slogans such as 'You get two weeks for being drunk and disorderly.' These billboard ads emphasize the unrestrained sun, sea, sand and sex image of the Club 18–30 holiday, encouraging the consumer to throw off all inhibitions. In fact the ads are slightly misleading in that the holidays are predominantly taken by men: the proportion of males to females on Club 18–30 holidays is around 2:1. This does not, of course, preclude those individuals from enjoying the sun, sea, sand and cheap alcohol.

On a rather more restrained level, the id is the main target of advertisements with a 'go on, spoil yourself' theme, such as most chocolate advertising. Products such as Alton Towers and Disneyland Paris appeal to the fun-seeking part of the *id*, and P&O Ferries play on P&O's reputation for luxury cruises to emphasize the pleasurable aspects of sailing across the Channel rather than using the Eurotunnel. For its part, Eurotunnel has to appeal to the practical *ego* by showing how much quicker and easier it is to use Le Shuttle.

Type approach

Freud was the earliest of the scientific psychologists. In subsequent years, additional beliefs to Freud's grew up. First came the followers of Jung, who (in addition to holding Freudian belief) also categorized people as *introverts* (preoccupied with themselves and the internal world) or *extroverts* (preoccupied with others and the outside world). This was an early attempt to classify people into broad types, and this process has continued ever since, with different researchers discovering different ways of grouping people according to personality types.

The mother and daughter team of Kathryn Briggs and Isabel Myers developed the Myers–Briggs Type Indicator[3] with four personality dimensions:

- Extrovert/introvert.
- Sensing/intuitive.
- Thinking/feeling.
- Judging/perceptive.

The combinations of these dimensions can define people into sixteen different types: for example, an extrovert-sensing-feeling-judging person is warm-hearted, talkative and popular, and likes harmonious relationships. An introvert-intuitive-thinking-judging person is likely to be quiet, intelligent, cerebral and reclusive.

Karen Horney[4] defined people across three dimensions:

- *Compliant*. Moves towards people, has goodness, sympathy, love, unselfishness and humility. Tends to be overapologetic, oversensitive, overgrateful, overgenerous and overconsiderate in seeking love and affection.
- *Aggressive*. Usually moves against people. Controls fears and emotions in a quest for success, prestige and admiration. Needs power, exploits others.
- *Detached*. Moves away from people. Conformity is repugnant to the detached person. Distrustful of others, these people are self-sufficient and independent, and value intelligence and reasoning.

There is some empirical evidence to show that these categorizations have some effect on people's buying behaviour. For example, it has been shown that compliant people use more mouthwash and toilet soap, and prefer branded products; aggressive people use more cologne and after-shave. Detached people show low interest in branding.[5]

David Reisman[6] categorized people against three categories:

- *Inner-directed* people are essentially driven from within, and are not too concerned with what other people think.
- *Other-directed* people get their motivation and take their cues from other people.

- *Tradition-directed* people get their cues and motivations from the past, from traditional beliefs and sources. These people are nowadays in a very tiny minority.

Reisman's categories have been used for marketing purposes. Inner-directeds, for example, tend to be innovators for cars and foodstuffs,[7] whereas outer-directeds have tended to be fashion victims.[8] There appears to be a change in the social paradigm, however, which is turning these views in a different direction. Broadly speaking, it would appear that more and more people are becoming inner-directed: according to some research-ers the current figure is around 40 per cent of the population.[9] This has led to a shift in the prevailing social paradigm away from the basically conformist attitude of the Victorian era towards a more individualistic, free-thinking society.

This shift in the social paradigm is having several effects. First, the fashion market has fragmented and almost anything goes.[10] Second, there is a declining respect for authority and an increase in the crime rate. Third, and more positive, there is an increase in the tendency for people to espouse causes and work towards altruistic goals, even in the face of opposition from the Establishment. The shift in the social paradigm is coming about as a result of increased wealth and security in the western world; as consumers move up Maslow's hierarchy of need (see Chapter 1) more of them are operating at the self-actualizing level.[11]

There is a clear parallel between Reisman's theory and the VALS model described in Chapter 1; the VALS model was in part derived from Reis-man's work.

Overall, the type approach has much to offer marketers. There is little doubt that personality type affects buying behaviour, and since such types are easily identified and appealed to through marketing communications, it is not difficult to approach these groups.

Traits and factors

Personality is composed of traits, or individual 'atoms' of personality. These individual predispositional attributes exert influences on behaviour, so the traits must be identified before people can be typed or classified.

Traits tend to be enduring facets of personality. In other words, traits tend not to change much over time, and even when they do change, they tend to do so rather slowly. Those that might tend to change with age are anxiety level (which tends to go down as the individual gets older), friendliness (which can change either way) and eagerness for novelty (which tends to go down).[12] A few traits may vary throughout life, but studies show that adult personalities do not vary significantly as a person ages. This is not to say that behaviour and attitudes do not change; merely that the underlying personality tends to stay very much the same. Changing roles, responsibilities and circumstances have much more effect on behaviour.

Traits can link to consumer behaviour. Research has shown that computer adopters in the early 1980s were more likely to be homebodies who thought of themselves as opinion leaders, were more intelligent than average, were cognitively structured (i.e. they thought a lot), and tended to be introverted and not socially active.[13] Presumably a similar study, if conducted in the 1990s, would show a different result since computer ownership is now so widespread.

The number of personality traits is very large indeed. There has been an estimate that there are almost 18,000 identifiable personality traits[14] and more are being discovered daily. Traits are clearly interrelated, but the study of this is still in its infancy, which is scarcely surprising given the number of traits that have been identified.

Currently the study of individual traits as they relate to buying behaviour is yielding few concrete results. This is probably because personality is interdependent; studying a few traits in isolation gives an insufficiently complete view of the whole person.[15]

Psychographics

Psychographics is sometimes known as lifestyle studies, since it is concerned with people's values and approaches to life. Essentially, it is a quantitative study of consumer lifestyles for the purpose of relating those lifestyles to the consumers' purchase behaviour. For example, somebody who has a 'green' set of values is likely to have an eco-friendly lifestyle, which in turn means that the individual will be more likely to buy a bike than a car, and more likely to be a vegetarian than eat red meat, and so forth. By knowing what a person's basic lifestyle is we can make a fair prediction as to hir or her purchasing behaviour, and the kind of products and promotions that will most appeal to that individual.

The psychographic approach to personality study combines the strengths of motivation research with those of trait and factor theories. The assessment of lifestyle often involves very lengthy and involved studies of large samples of the population: the Target Group Index annual research programme, which is run by BMRB, asks people to respond to 246 lifestyle statements. From this survey, different lifestyles can be identified and consequently different purchasing patterns can be predicted.

Table 3.2 UK lifestyles

	Lifestyle type	Characteristics	% of population
Sustenance-driven groups; motivated by the need for security	Belonger	People who believe in the establishment, traditional family values and patriotism. Averse to change.	19
	Survivor	People who are fighting a 'holding action'; accepts authority, hard working, quiet, traditional. Strong class consciousness.	16
	Aimless	Two main categories: the young unemployed whose main motivation is short-term 'kicks', and the very old, whose motivation is simply day-to-day existence.	5
Outer-directed group	Conspicuous consumer	Interested in material possessions, taking cues from reference groups (friends, family). Followers of fashion.	18
Inner-directed groups; motivated by self-actualization	Social resister	Caring group, motivated by ideals of fairness and a good quality of life at the societal level. Altruistic, concerned with social issues like ecology and nuclear disarmament.	11
	Experimentalists	Materialistic and pro-technology, individualistic and interested in novelty.	14
	Self-explorers	Motivated by self-expression and self-realization. Tolerant, able to think big and look for global, holistic solutions.	16

Source: Adapted from W. Kirk McNulty, 'UK social change through a wide-angle lens' *Futures*, August 1985.

An example of this approach is the VALS breakdown referred to in Chapter 1. A UK equivalent was developed by Taylor Nelson, with the groups as shown in Table 3.2.

Psychographics approaches have in common that they all try to predict behaviour from knowledge of lifestyle and attitudes. The drawback with this approach is that the necessary research is complex and time consuming, and ultimately relies heavily on the judgement of the researchers to decide which factors are appropriate to a particular lifestyle. For example, is somebody who uses unleaded petrol really living a 'green' lifestyle? Presumably a truly 'green' lifestyle would not involve a car at all!

The psychographics approach appears to have strong potential to tell us about what people will buy, since clearly most purchases are related to a chosen lifestyle. The problem is therefore not conceptual, but rather one of definition.

Self-concept

'Of all the personality concepts which have been applied to marketing, self-concept has probably provided the most consistent results and the greatest promise of application to the needs of business firms' (Gordon Foxall).[16]

Self-concept is the person's ideas and feelings about him or herself. It has an important role to play in understanding consumer behaviour, since people will buy products which contribute to the self-concept. For example, a woman who thinks of herself as a *femme fatale* will choose chic clothes to enhance that image; or a man who thinks of himself as a handyman will equip himself with the most sophisticated tools.

Essentially, people project a role and this is confirmed (or denied) by the people around. In order for the role to be confirmed, the person will try to develop all the exterior accoutrements appropriate to the role. In this sense, the person becomes a work of art; a sensory stimulus to other people which is intended to generate affective responses. The person may well use all five senses to generate the affective response: sight (by dressing appropriately, wearing make-up, etc.), hearing (by speaking with the right accent, or using the voice well), smell (by wearing perfume or deodorant), touch (by looking after the skin, perhaps by wearing clothes that feel good) and even taste (flavoured lipstick, mouthwashes).

Some of these sensory stimuli will, of course, be available only to the individual's closest friends, and often only to lovers, but most people at some time or another will consciously set out to create a work of art of themselves in order to 'make a good impression' on somebody. The extent to which people do this depends on the following factors:

- The degree of importance attached to impressing the other person (or people).
- The degree to which the individual anticipates that the 'target audience' can be impressed.
- The cost in time and money of creating the desired image.

Clearly, though, the fact that people do create these works of art has led to the invention of whole industries to cater for the need: the cosmetics industry and fashion industry, to name but two.

Self-concept is a learned construct. Children tend to look for role-models to imitate; these may not always be the same people, and the child may try several different role-models before settling on one that is appropriate. Children can be crushed by a denial of the role being projected: for example, if people laugh while the child is imitating a favourite auntie or uncle. During the teenage years, a further refinement occurs as the individual tries to develop an adult role, and again the role-models may shift, typically away from the family members towards a hero (pop star or sporting personality) or sometimes to an individual within a peer group (a school friend, for example). Usually the role-model will be an adult a few years older.

Self-concept has four attributes, as follows:

- It is learned, not innate.
- It is stable and consistent. Self-perception may change; self-concept does not. This accounts for brand loyalty, since self-concept involves a view of which products will 'fit the image'.
- It is purposeful: in other words, there is a reason and a purpose behind it. Essentially, self-concept is there to protect and enhance a person's ego. It is therefore advisable not to attack a person's beliefs directly; people get angry or at least defensive when this happens.
- The self-concept is unique to the individual, and promotes individualism.

Self-image breaks down into different components, or dimensions.[17] These are shown in Table 3.3. There is some overlap, but the differences are quite marked between the dimensions. Each dimension has some relevance for marketers, and the implications are as shown in Table 3.4.

For marketers, the differences are useful. Ideal self predicts attempts at upward mobility: purchases of courses, self-improvement classes, upmarket

Table 3.3 Components of self-image

Component	Explanation
Real self	This is the actual, objective self, as others see us. There is a problem with this definition, since other people never know the whole story. This means that the 'real' self may be something other than the face shown to the world.
Self-image	This is the subjective self, as we see ourselves. Self-image is likely to differ radically from the real self, but to an extent this is modified over time because of feedback from others. We modify our self-image in the light of the reactions of others.
Ideal self	How we wish we were; this connects to the self-actualization need that Maslow identified. This self is often the one that provokes the most extravagant spending, as the individual tries to make up the gap between self-image and ideal self.
Looking-glass self	The social self, or the way we think other people see us. This does not always coincide with the way people actually see us, since we are not able to read minds. Feedback from others will be constrained by politeness or by a desire to project a self-image on the part of the respondent, so we are not always aware of what other people really think we are like.

Table 3.4 Dimensions of self-image

Dimension	Relevance to marketers	Examples
Real self	As the face that is shown to the world, this is the one that people most wish to influence.	Conspicuous consumption of cars, houses, etc. Cosmetics, fashion and hairdressing.
Self-image	Useful in two ways: first, the negative aspects of self-image influence the ideal self; second, the positive aspects influence purchases to reinforce the self-image.	Somebody whose self-image is 'cool' will not want to jeopardize that, and will buy appropriate products to match that image. Somebody whose self-image is poor will want to correct discrepancies.
Ideal self	The aspect that leads to the greatest purchases of self-improvement products.	Correspondence courses, cosmetics, cosmetic surgery, musical instruments and any number of other products that lead to self-development.
Looking-glass self	The way we *think* others see us; this influences us in making changes to those views, or reinforcing views that are perceived as positive.	A man who thinks his friends see him as being staid or boring might be prompted to buy a sports car in order to correct the image. Conversely, somebody more outer directed might deliberately buy a car to fit in with the image he thinks he has with his friends; perhaps a Ford Escort or Vauxhall Nova because his friends see him as a solid, down-to-earth person.

products, cosmetic surgery, etc. Looking-glass self is relevant for other-directed people.

Self-image is relevant to what we think we deserve; what is the 'right' product for us. People are swayed by what is promoted as being 'just right for people like you' – children can be told they are having 'the special children's meal'; students can be swayed by a 'special student discount', OAPs by the special 'senior citizen's service'. Sometimes this type of promotion can backfire – there may be fears about the quality of the service or product, for instance.

Real self is not known to the consumer, although it is one of the greatest motivators in consumer behaviour. In the words of Burns, 'To see ourselves as others see us' is not in our gift – and this may be just as well.

Referring back to Goffman's life-as-theatre analogy, it is clear that purchases of props and costume are relevant to the real self. Developing a real self which is positive and useful to us is done via feedback from others (applause) and by acting appropriately.

Achieving the ideal self is very much about getting appropriate applause and critical acclaim, so that we know whether we are getting it right; but perhaps more importantly there is the element of learning the lines and getting the production right in terms of costume, make-up and script. People therefore modify their behaviour according to the feedback obtained; this is called *self-monitoring*.[18] Self-monitoring has three forms of expression: concern for the appropriateness of behaviour, attention to social comparison as cues for appropriate self-expression, and the ability to modify self-presentation and expression across situations.[19]

In other words, people ensure that their behaviour is appropriate for the occasion by observing what others are doing and by acting in harmony with that behaviour. Rather like the inexperienced diner who watches others to see which knife and fork to use for each course, people take cues from those around them in order to ensure polite behaviour. Low self-monitors are more likely to behave according to some inner drive, and may even prefer to be seen as being different from the rest of humanity; high self-monitors are more likely to conform with those around them, and are therefore more susceptible to appeals to be fashionable.

Key points from this chapter

In this chapter we have looked at what constitutes people's personalities and self-concept. We have also looked at role playing in terms of Goffman's life-as-theatre analogy, and at some of the ways in which these elements affect consumers' buying behaviour. Car manufacturers still sell on personality: recent examples are the series of TV advertisements for the Renault Clio, and perfumes such as Tramp and Calvin Klein.

Many petfood advertisements also rely on personality. The Kit-E-Kat cat is lively, inquisitive, a little mischievous and always affectionate to its human. The implication is that feeding the cat Kit-E-Kat will make it into this type of cat, even if it starts out as a less-than-perfect housepet.

Here are the key points of the chapter:

- Role playing is subconscious, not a conscious decision to deceive.
- Personality is made up of traits; so far 18,000 possible traits have been identified.
- Personality is a self-serving, individualistic, unique, overt and consistent *Gestalt*.
- Self-concept is concerned with one's feelings about oneself.
- Self-concept is learned, stable, purposeful and unique.

- High self-monitors take their cues from others; low self-monitors take their cues from an inner drive.

Notes

1. Erving Goffman, *The Presentation of Self in Everyday Life* (Harmondsworth: Penguin, 1969).
2. Elizabeth C. Hirschmann and Morris B. Holbrook, 'Hedonic consumption: emerging concepts, methods and propositions', *Journal of Marketing*, vol. 46 (Summer 1982), pp. 91–101.
3. Kathryn Briggs and Isabel Myers, 'The Myers–Briggs Type Indicator', *San Jose Mercury News*, 23 September 1992.
4. Karen Horney, *Our Inner Conflict*, (New York: W.W. Norton, 1945).
5. Joel B. Cohen, 'An interpersonal orientation to the study of consumer behaviour', *Journal of Marketing Research*, vol. 4 (August 1967), pp. 270–8.
6. David Reisman, *The Lonely Crowd* (New York: Doubleday 1953).
7. James H. Donnelly, Jr., 'Social character and acceptance of new products', *Journal of Marketing Research*, vol. 7 (February 1970), pp. 111–13.
8. George M. Zinkhan and Ali Shermohamad, 'Is other-directedness on the increase? An empirical test of Reisman's theory of social character', *Journal of Consumer Research*, vol. 13 (June 1986), pp. 127–30.
9. W. Kirk McNulty, 'UK social change through a wide-angle lens', *Futures*, August 1985.
10. Martin Evans and Jim Blythe; 'Fashion: a new paradigm of consumer behaviour', *Journal of Consumer Studies and Home Economics*, vol. 18 (1994), pp. 229–37.
11. McNulty, *op. cit.*
12. Daniel Goleman, 'Basic personality traits don't change, studies say', *New York Times*, 18 June 1987.
13. Mary Lee Dickerson and James W. Gentry, 'Characteristics of adopters and non-adopters of home computers', *Journal of Consumer Research*, vol. 10 (September 1983), pp. 225–35.
14. G.W. Allport and H.S. Odbert, 'Trait names: a psycholexial study', Psychological Monograph 47, no. 211 (1936).
15. *Marketing News*, 13 September 1985, p. 56.
16. Gordon Foxall, *Consumer Behaviour; A practical guide* (London: Routledge, 1980).
17. Beth Ann Walker, 'New perspectives for self-research', in John H. Sherry, Jr, and Brian Sternthal (eds.), *Advances in Consumer Research*, vol. 19 (Provo, UT: Association for Consumer Research, 1992).
18. Mark Snyder, 'Self-monitoring of expressive behaviour', *Journal of Personality and Social Psychology*, vol. 34 (1974), pp. 526–37.
19. Jacques Nantel and William Strahle, 'The self-monitoring concept: a consumer perspective', in Richard E. Lutz (ed.), *Advances in Consumer Research*, vol. 13 (Provo, UT: Association for Consumer Research, 1986).

4

Learning and perception

This chapter is about the ways in which the brain selects, orders and stores information. When you have read this chapter, you should be able to:

- Explain the ways in which people select information from the environment.
- Describe and contrast some theories of learning.
- Suggest ways in which learning theory can be applied in a marketing context.
- Explain the role of advertising in learning.
- Explain the analytic and synthetic processes of perception.

Learning

Learning is not only about classroom-type learning. Most behaviour is learned as a result of external experiences; most of what people know (and almost certainly many of the things they are most proud of knowing) they learned outside school. People learn things partly through a formalized structure of teaching (or of self-teaching, perhaps by correspondence course) and partly through an unconscious process of learning by experience.

Consumption habits particularly are learned. British people were not born with a liking for fish and chips, any more than a Korean is born with a liking for boiled dog, or a Frenchman for horsemeat. Learning is highly relevant to marketing, since consumers are affected by the things they learn, and much consumer behaviour is actually based on the learning process.

Persuading consumers to remember the information they see in advertisements is a major problem for marketers. For example, some years ago a series of advertisements were produced for Cinzano vermouth. The ads starred Leonard Rossiter and Joan Collins, and were widely screened throughout the UK, yet they were ineffective in increasing sales of the product. The reason for this was made clear when market research discovered that consumers actually thought the ads were for Martini vermouth, Cinzano's main competitor.

Learning is defined as *the behavioural changes that occur over time relative to an external stimulus condition.*[1] According to this definition, activities are changed or originated through a reaction to an encountered situation. We can therefore say that someone has learned something if, as a result, the person's behaviour changes in some way.

The main conditions that arise from this definition are as follows:

- There must be a change in behaviour (response tendencies).
- This must result from external stimulus.

Learning has *not* taken place under the following circumstances:

- *Species' response tendencies.* These are instincts, or reflexes: for example, the response of ducking when a stone is thrown at you does not rely on your having learned that stones are hard and hurt the skin. Learning has not taken place under those circumstances.
- *Maturation.* Behavioural changes often occur in adolescence due to hormonal changes (for example), but again this is not a behavioural change as a result of learning.
- *Temporary states of the organism.* While behaviour can be, and often is, affected by tiredness, hunger, drunkenness, etc., these factors do not constitute part of a larger learning process (even though learning may result from those states; the drunk may well learn to drink less in future).

Regarding the study of learning, there are two main schools of thought: first, the stimulus–response approach, which further subdivides into classical and operant conditioning; and second, cognitive theories, where the conscious thought of the individual enters into the equation.

Classical learning theory

The classical theory of learning was developed by, among others, the Russian researcher Pavlov.[2] Pavlov's famous experiments with dogs demonstrated that automatic responses (reflexes) could be learned. What Pavlov did was present a dog with an unconditioned stimulus (in this case, meat), knowing that this would lead to an unconditioned response (salivation). At the same time, Pavlov would ring a bell (the conditioned stimulus). After a while the dog would associate the ringing of the bell with the meat, and would salivate whenever it heard the bell, without actually seeing any meat. This mechanism is shown in Figure 4.1.

Classical conditioning like this occurs with humans. Many smokers associate having a cup of coffee with having a cigarette, and find it difficult to give up smoking without also giving up coffee. Likewise the use of popular music in the Levi's ads is an example of classical conditioning. Repeated exposure to the advertisement leads the individual to associate the music with the product. This gives two results: first, if the consumer likes the music, that extends to liking the product; and second, the consumer will tend to think of Levi's whenever she or he hears the music. Assuming the song used actually becomes (or is already) a hit, Levi will obtain some free exposure whenever the song is played on the radio. Likewise, Christmas music played in retail shops during December tends to get consumers in the mood to buy presents and seasonal items.

For this to work, it is usually necessary to repeat the stimulus a number of times in order for the conditioned response to become established. The number of times the process needs to be repeated will depend on the strength of the stimulus and the receptiveness (motivation) of the individual. Research has shown that, although conditioning has been reported for

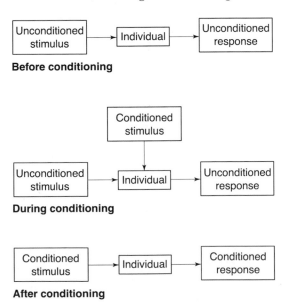

Figure 4.1 Classical conditioning

a single conditioning event,[3] as many as 30 pairings may be required before conditioning is maximized.[4]

Before conditioning, the unconditioned stimulus feeding into the brain causes the unconditioned response. During the conditioning, both the conditioned stimulus and the unconditioned stimulus are presented, so that after conditioning the conditioned stimulus alone will produce the response.

Behaviours influenced by classical conditioning are thought to be involuntary. If the doorbell rings, it is automatic for most people to look up, without consciously thinking about whether somebody is at the door. Most people are familiar with the start of recognition that sometimes occurs if a similar doorbell is rung during a TV drama. Classical conditioning also operates on the emotions: playing Christmas music will elicit memories of childhood Christmases, and ads evoking nostalgic feelings (such as the Hovis ads) will generate warm feelings towards the product.

Another factor in the effectiveness of classical conditioning is the order in which the conditioned stimulus and the unconditioned stimulus are presented. In *forward conditioning*, the conditioned stimulus (CS) comes before the unconditioned stimulus (US). This means that the product would be shown before the music was played.

In *backward conditioning*, the US comes before the CS. Here the music would be played before the product is shown. *Simultaneous conditioning* requires both to be presented at the same time.

It appears that forward conditioning and simultaneous conditioning work best in advertising.[5] This means that it is usually better to present the product before playing the popular tune, or play both together; the responses from this approach are usually stronger and longer lasting. If classical conditioning is being used, clearly the broadcast media such as TV and radio will be better suited, since it is easier to control the order in which the stimuli are presented; with print media this is not necessarily the case. For example, not everybody reads newspapers from front to back. Many people would start with the sports pages (at the back) and work forward, or perhaps read the headlines on the front pages, then go straight to the TV pages before coming back to the local news. Even if the conditioned stimulus and unconditioned stimulus are placed in the same ad on the same page, it is still possible that the reader's eye will be drawn to each stimulus in the wrong order: people do not necessarily read each page from top to bottom, either.

Extinction occurs when the conditioned stimulus no longer evokes the conditioned response. This occurs in the ways shown in Table 4.1.

Generalization happens when a stimulus that is close to the existing one evokes the same response. Pavlov found that a sound similar to the bell he used could also stimulate salivation, and it is often the case that a similar brand name can evoke a purchase response. A very common tactic in

Table 4.1 Routes by which extinction occurs

Reason for extinction	Example	Explanation	Techniques to avoid extinction
The conditioned stimulus is encountered without the unconditioned stimulus.	The product is shown without the background music.	Seeing the product without the music tends to reduce the association of the music with the product; other stimuli will replace the music.	Ensure that all the advertising uses the same music, or imagery associated with the music.
The unconditioned stimulus is encountered without the conditioned stimulus.	The background music is heard without the product being present.	In this case, other stimuli may be evoked by the music; it will become associated with something other than the product.	Either ensure that the music is not played anywhere other than when the product is being shown, or ensure that the product is available when the music is played. For example, ensure that the disco has an ample supply of the drink you are advertising.

marketing is to produce similar packaging to that of one's competitor in order to take advantage of the generalization effect. For an example of this, observe the similarity in the packaging between Tesco's Premium coffee and Nescafé Gold Blend.

Discrimination is the process by which we learn to distinguish between stimuli, and only respond to the appropriate one. Consumers quite quickly learn to distinguish between brands, even when the design of the packaging is similar. Advertisers will often encourage discrimination by pairing a positive US with their own product, but not with the competitor's product: for example, the Heineken slogan, 'Refreshes the parts other beers cannot reach'. Even greater discrimination occurs when the competitor's product is paired with a negative US, as in the current Daewoo marketing campaign, where the company has compared its own approach to dealer training and after-sales support with the less-than-ideal approaches of other car manufacturers and dealers. The campaign has been so effective that the company has been banned from some motor shows.[6]

Classical conditioning is responsible for many repetitive advertising campaigns, and for many catchphrases which are now in common use. Some advertising fosters this, as in the 'I bet he drinks Carling Black Label' campaign, which has resulted in the slogan entering the language. In some cases these stimuli can be very long lasting: the depiction of Santa Claus dressed in red and white is the result of a Coca-Cola campaign from the early part of this century, Santa having previously been dressed in green.

Classical conditioning assumes that the individual plays no active role in the learning process. Pavlov's dogs did not have to do anything in order to be 'conditioned', because the process was carried out on their involuntary reflex of salivation. Although classical conditioning does operate in human beings, people are not usually passive in the process: the individual person (and most higher animals, in fact) is able to take part in the process and co-operate with it or avoid it. This process of active role playing is called *operant conditioning*.

Operant conditioning

Here the learner will conduct trial-and-error behaviour to obtain a reward (or avoid a punishment). Burris F. Skinner[7] developed the concept in order to explain higher-level learning than that identified by Pavlov. The difference between Pavlov's approach and the operant conditioning approach is that the learner has choice in the outcome; the modern view of classical conditioning is that it also involves a cognitive dimension. In other words, Skinner is describing a type of learning that requires the learner to do something rather than be a passive recipient of a stimulus; and the modern view is that even Pavlov's dog would have thought 'Here comes dinner' when the bell rang.

The basis of operant conditioning is the concept of reinforcement. If a consumer buys a product and is pleased with the outcome of using it, then he or she is likely to buy the product again. This means that the activity has had a positive reinforcement, and the consumer has become 'conditioned' to buy the product next time. The greater the positive reinforcement, the greater the likelihood of repeat purchase.

If the reward works, the consumer will try to think of a way to make it even better. 'If a little will help, a lot will cure.' This can lead to over-indulgence in food or alcohol, or indeed almost any other pleasurable activity. Typically this will happen if the consumer's need cannot be totally met by the product, but will be helped: a person with a serious psycho-logical problem may well find that alcohol helps, but does not cure. An increasing intake of alcohol will never result in a complete meeting of the person's psychological needs because eventually sobriety will begin to set in again.

An example of operant conditioning is the recent growth of loyalty cards in retail stores: for example, Tesco's Clubcard. Customers who remain loyal to Tesco get extra discounts and offers, and also (eventually) their purchasing behaviour can be traced through the electronic point-of-sale systems so that offers can be targeted to those Tesco customers who will really be interested in them.

Airline loyalty schemes have also seen huge growth in recent years. These are aimed at reinforcing the frequent flyers, whose loyalty is desirable since they are likely to be the most profitable customers. The airlines offer free flights to their most regular customers, and for many business travellers these free flights offer an attractive reason for choosing the same airline every time.

On the other hand, an overuse of incentives can lead to negative consequences for the producer. An example is Pizzaland's discount vouchers, which have been given away in newspapers, on bus tickets and even on cans of tuna. The result of this is that many people will not eat at Pizzaland unless they have a discount voucher. In this way, the positive reinforcement has backfired on the company, since there is an implied *negative* reinforcement in *not* going in with a voucher.

Figure 4.2 charts three forms of operant conditioning. In the first example, positive reinforcement, the individual receives a stimulus and acts upon it. This action works, and the individual gets a good result; this leads to the behaviour being repeated if the same antecedent stimulus is presented at a later date. For example, if you are in a long queue at B&Q, you might notice that the Customer Service counter is empty, and go there to make your purchases instead of the usual tills. This gets you through quicker, so if you are in B&Q again and the queue is overlong, you try the same tactic again.

The second example in the diagram shows a negative stimulus. This time the operant behaviour relieves the problem, and again the individual has learned how to avoid bad consequences when faced with a difficulty.

The third example shows how punishment fits into the learning process. If the operant behaviour leads to a bad result – for example, the Customer Service counter will not serve you and you lose your original place in the queue, you will not try that tactic again. The problem with punishment as a motivator is that it may lead to the individual not shopping at B&Q again (see Chapter 1 for a further discussion of pain avoidance).

Operant conditioning does not necessarily require a product purchase: marketers will frequently give away free samples in the hope that a positive experience from using the product will encourage consumers to purchase in future. Likewise, car dealers always offer a test drive; some go even further, and allow the customer to borrow a car for 24 hours or more in order to get a very clear reinforcement of the car's merits.

Operant conditioning is helpful in explaining how people become conditioned, or form habits of purchase; however, it still does not explain how learning operates when people become active in seeking out information.

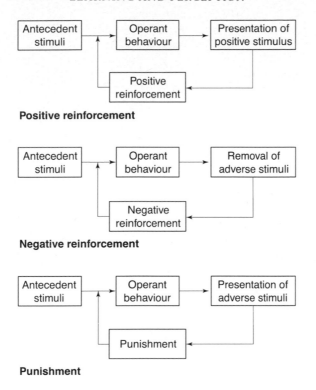

Positive reinforcement

Negative reinforcement

Punishment

Figure 4.2 Forms of operant conditioning (Source: Adapted from Stanley M. Widrick, 'Concept of negative reinforcement has place in classroom', *Marketing News*, 18 July 1986, pp. 48–9)

To understand this aspect of learning, it is necessary to look at the cognitive learning process.

Cognitive learning

Not all learning is just an automatic response to a stimulus. People analyze purchasing situations taking into account previous experiences, and make evaluative judgements. Learning is part of this, both in terms of informing the process as a result of earlier experiences, and also in terms of the consumer's approach to learning more about the product category or brand.

When considering cognitive learning, the emphasis is not on *what* is learned (as in stimulus–response theories), but on *how* it is learned. Classical learning and operant conditioning theories suppose that learning is

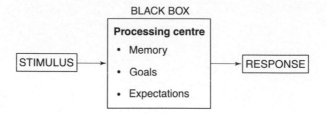

Figure 4.3 Model of learning process

automatic; cognitive learning theories assume that there is a conscious process going on. For most people this is true in many cases of consumer behaviour.

The classical and operant theories assume that what goes on inside the consumer's head is a 'black box', in that we know that a given stimulus will prompt a particular response, but for most practical purposes we have no real way of knowing what is happening inside the black box. Within the cognitive learning paradigm, however, we are concerned with what happens inside the box, and we try to infer what is going on by analyzing behaviour and responses from the individual. Figure 4.3 illustrates this.

The black box contains the cognitive processes; the stimulus is considered in the light of the individual's memory of what has happened in the past when presented with similar stimuli, his or her assessment of the desirable outcome, and an assessment of the likely outcome of any action. Following this processing, the individual produces a response.

Cognitive learning expertise has five aspects:

- Cognitive effort.
- Cognitive structure.
- Analysis.
- Elaboration.
- Memory.

Cognitive effort is the degree of effort the consumer is prepared to put into thinking about the product offering. This will depend on such aspects as the complexity of the product, the consumer's involvement with it, and the motivation for learning.

Cognitive structure is about the way the consumer thinks, and the way the information is fitted into the existing knowledge.

The *analysis* of information is concerned, first, with selecting the correct, relevant information from the environment, and second, with interpreting the information correctly in order to obtain a clear action plan.

Elaboration is the structuring of the information within the brain, and adding to it from memory in order to form a coherent whole.

Memory is the mechanism by which learned information is stored. In fact, nothing is ever truly forgotten: information will eventually become irrecoverable by the conscious mind (forgotten), but the brain still retains the information and can be stimulated to recall it, either by hypnosis or by association of ideas.

Cognitive learning processes are important to marketers, since they are helpful in predicting consumer responses to advertising. Stephen J. Hoch and Young-Won Ha[8] say that consumers view advertisements as tentative hypotheses about product performance that can be tested through product experience. Early learning about a product will affect future learning; this is called the *law of primacy.* For this reason, first impressions count for a great deal.

According to Stephen Hoch and Young-Won Ha, advertising will tend to be ignored if there is unambiguous objective evidence to hand: if you can test the product for yourself, the adverts will not affect you as much. If the evidence is ambiguous or unobtainable at first hand (as is often the case), the advertising might sway you, and in fact advertising appears to have dramatic effects on consumers' perceptions of quality.

For example, it is possible for somebody to test out a new computer before making a commitment to buy. Thus advertising plays a small part in computer purchase, only serving to alert the consumer to what is available within the current technology. Conversely, somebody spending a similar amount on a holiday has no chance to try out the holiday before buying it, and is therefore more likely to be swayed by the advertising or other communications (brochures, salespeople, etc.) One of the main considerations for a consumer in this position is the reputation of the tour operator, since the consumer is, after all, buying a promise. Chapter 11 has more on the topic of services marketing.

Learning from experience is a four-stage process, as Table 4.2 shows. In most cases, people prefer to learn by experience, especially for major product purchases. Few people would buy a car without having a test drive first, and still fewer would buy one by mail order unless they had previous direct experience of the car. It is for this reason that mail-order companies have a no-quibble money-back guarantee; if this were not the case, few people would be prepared to buy by post rather than visit a High Street shop where they can see and feel the goods.

There are also three moderating factors in the cognitive learning process:

- *Familiarity* with the domain. This is the degree to which the consumer has pre-existing knowledge of the product category. For example, a computer buff would go through a different, and probably shorter, learning curve for buying a new type of machine than would a complete novice.

Table 4.2 Stages of learning by experience

Stage	Explanation	Example	Marketing response
Hypothesizing	Developing a rough estimate of what is happening or what is available	Getting information from a friend, or reading some advertising material; getting some brochures	Have clearly written brochures and advertising; do not use too much jargon, especially if your product is a complex one, or can be 'test-driven'.
Exposure	Having a look at the product, trying one out, getting direct experience of it	Visiting a computer shop to try the product and ask questions about it	Ensure that the product is on display, and allow plenty of opportunity for hands-on testing.
Encoding	Making sense of the information	Translating the jargon into something comprehensible, perhaps getting some clarification; understanding what the product is and does in terms which fit in with previous experience	Have salespeople who can explain things in lay terms, and who do not frighten the customer off by using too much technical language.
Integration	Fitting the new information into the existing knowledge bank	Thinking about the new information gained about computers and discarding previous misconceptions	Ensure that customers feel able to come back for further explanations if they still have problems. Make sure that customers understand everything before leaving the shop.

- *Motivation* to learn. If the purchase is an important one, or the possible effects of making a mistake are serious, the consumer is likely to be highly motivated to obtain as much information as possible.
- *Ambiguity* of the information environment. If the information is hard to get, contradictory or incomprehensible, this will hinder the learning process. Sometimes consumers give up on the process if this is the case.

Table 4.3 uses these moderating factors to classify readiness to learn from experience.

Cognitive theories recognize that consumers influence the outcome in an active manner, so the learning process is not always easy for an outsider (i.e. a marketing person) to manage. This may be part of the reason why new products fail so frequently: weak motivation to learn about new products leads to difficulty for marketers in starting the learning process.

Cognitive learning has five elements, as follows:

- *Drive*. As seen in Chapter 2, drive is the stimulus that impels action. It is strong, internal and general. The impulse to learn can be driven by a fear

Table 4.3 Managing the learning process

How motivated are consumers to learn?	What do consumers already know?	How much can experience teach?	
		Little (high ambiguity)	A lot (low ambiguity)
Highly motivated	Unfamiliar	Learning is most susceptible to management.	Learning is spontaneous, rapid and difficult to manage.
	Familiar	Formation of superstitious beliefs is possible. Existing beliefs inhibit suggestibility.	
Weakly motivated	Unfamiliar	Learning is slow to start and difficult to sustain, but is susceptible to management.	Learning is difficult to initiate and once started difficult to manage.
	Familiar	Complacency inhibits initiation of learning, so experience is unresponsive to management.	

Source: Stephen J. Hoch and John Deighton, 'Managing what consumers learn from experience', *Journal of Marketing*, vol. 53 (April 1989), pp. 1–20.

of making an expensive mistake, or by a desire to maximize the benefits of the purchase.

- *Cue*. This is an external trigger which encourages learning. It is weaker than a drive, is external, and is specific. For example, a public service such as the Health and Safety Council might exhort employers to send for a leaflet on safety in the workplace. Sometimes firms will use advertisement retrieval cues to trigger responses.
- *Response*. This is the reaction of the consumer to the interaction between a drive and a cue. With luck, this results in a sale; but humans learn, and will base future purchases on their concrete experience of the product rather than on the marketer's cues.
- *Reinforcement*. Purchase response should be rewarded with a positive experience of the product. The object of reinforcement is to get consumers to associate the product with certain benefits. An example is the servicing policy of Daewoo cars, by which each car comes with three years' servicing. This means that the customer knows that any problems with the car will be fixed immediately, and thus the experience of owning the Daewoo is likely to be positive. From Daewoo's viewpoint the positive experience of the customer, and therefore the likelihood of repeat sales, is worth the cost and trouble of providing the servicing, rather than allowing customers to choose their own, possibly unreliable, servicing option.
- *Retention*. This is the stability of the learned material over time, or in other words how well it is remembered. Advertising jingles have very

high retention. Consumers can often recall jingles that have not been broadcast for 30 years or more. This is particularly true for advertisements that were popular when the consumer was a child. (The opposite of retention is *extinction*).

Learned responses are never truly unlearned. The brain *remembers* (stores) everything, but rather like a computer with a faulty disk drive it may not always be able to *recall* (retrieve) everything. Also, the human memory is huge: the *Encyclopaedia Britannica* contains 12,500 million characters, but the brain has 125,000,000 million characters' storage capacity. This is enough storage to hold 10,000 *Encyclopaedia Britannicas*, which makes the human brain easily the world's most powerful computer.[9]

Perception

Human beings have considerably more than five senses. Apart from the basic five (touch, taste, smell, sight, hearing) there are senses of direction, the sense of balance, a clear knowledge of which way is down, and so forth. Each sense is feeding information to the brain constantly, and the amount of information being collected would seriously overload the system if one took it all in. The brain therefore selects from the environment around the individual and cuts out the extraneous noise.

In effect, the brain makes automatic decisions as to what is relevant and what is not. Even though there may be many things happening around you, you are unaware of most of them; in fact, experiments have shown that some information is filtered out by the optic nerve even before it gets to the brain. People quickly learn to ignore extraneous noises: for example, as a visitor to someone else's home you may be sharply aware of a loudly ticking clock, whereas your host may be entirely used to it, and unaware of it except when making a conscious effort to check that the clock is still running.

Therefore the information entering the brain does not provide a complete view of the world around you.

When the individual constructs a world-view, he or she then assembles the remaining information to map what is happening in the outside world. Any gaps (and there will, of course, be plenty of these) will be filled in with imagination and experience. The cognitive map is therefore not a 'photograph'; it is a construct of the imagination. This mapping will be affected by the following factors:

- *Subjectivity*. This is the existing world-view within the individual, and is unique to that individual.

- *Categorization*. This is the 'pigeonholing' of information, and the pre-judging of events and products. This can happen through a process known as *chunking*, whereby the individual organizes information into chunks of related items.[10] For example, a picture seen while a particular piece of music is playing might be chunked as one item in the memory, so that sight of the picture evokes the music and vice versa.
- *Selectivity*. This is the degree to which the brain is selecting from the environment. It is a function of how much is going on around the individual, and also of how selective (concentrated) the individual is on the current task. Selectivity is also subjective: some people are a great deal more selective than others.
- *Expectations*. These lead individuals to interpret later information in a specific way. For example, look at this series of numbers and letters:

𝒜 ℬ 𝒞 𝒟 ℰ ℱ 𝒢 ℌ 𝒥

10 11 12 13 14 15 16

In fact, the number 13 appears in both series, but in the first series it would be interpreted as a B because that is what the brain is being led to expect. (The B in Matura MT Script looks like this: ℬ.)

- *Past experience*. This leads us to interpret later experience in the light of what we already know. Psychologists call this the law of primacy. Sometimes sights, smells or sounds from our past will trigger off inappropriate responses: the smell of bread baking may recall a village bakery from twenty years ago, but in fact the smell could have been artificially generated by an aerosol spray near the supermarket bread counter.

An example of cognitive mapping as applied to perception of product quality might run as follows. The consumer uses the input selector to select clues and assign values to them. For quality, the cues are typically price, brand name and retailer name. There are strong positive relationships between price and quality in most consumers' perceptions, and brand name and quality; although the retailer name is less significant, it still carries some weight. For example, many consumers would feel confident that Harrod's would sell higher-quality items than the local corner shop, but might be less able to distinguish between Sainsbury's and Tesco's.

The information is *subjective* in that the consumer will base decisions on the selected information. Each of us selects differently from the environment, and each of us has differing views.

Information about quality will be pigeonholed, or *categorized*: the individual may put Jaguar in the same category as BMW, or perhaps put Sony in the same slot as Hitachi.

Selectivity will depend on how much is going on in the environment, on the individual's interest and motivation regarding the subject area, and on the degree of concentration the individual has on the task in hand. People with a highly developed ability to concentrate select less from the environment because they are able to 'shut out' the world much more.

Expectations of quality play a huge part: if the individual is expecting a high-quality item, he or she will select evidence which supports that view and tend to ignore evidence that does not.

Past experience will also play a part in quality judgement. If the consumer has had bad experiences of Japanese products, this might lead to a general perception that Japanese products are poor quality.

Price also has a strong effect on people's view of quality. There is a general belief that the higher the price, the better the quality in some way. Often this view will be justified, of course. The downside from a marketer's viewpoint is that price has a negative effect on perceived value and on willingness to buy. The problem lies in knowing how big a price reduction will increase sales without leading to a negative perception of quality.

Weber's Law states that the size of the least detectable change depends on the size of the stimulus. This means that a very intense stimulus will require a bigger change if the change is to be perceived by the consumer. For example, 3p off the price of a morning newspaper is a substantial discount, and would attract attention in advertising; 3p off the price of a BMW would go unnoticed. Clearly at this level of intensity (a price of a few pence compared with a price of thousands of pounds) Weber's Law may not work very precisely,[11] but in the middle range of prices the law appears to work well. Incidentally, reducing the price from £10 to £9.99 is very noticeable even though the actual reduction is only 0.1 per cent of the initial price. The important element here is that the reduction is noticeable.

Weber's Law also applies to product differentiation. The law can be applied to determine how much better the product has to be for the difference to be noticeable,[12] or conversely to determine how similar the product needs to be, to be indistinguishable from the leading brand.

It should be noted here that perception and reality are not different things. There is a popular view that perception somehow differs from reality; in fact, reality only exists in the heads of individuals. If there is an objective reality, it is not accessible to us as human beings; we only have what our senses tell us, and for each of us reality is different because each of us selects and synthesizes in a different way. Figure 4.4 may help to illustrate this.

The individual in the diagram is in a crowded room, yet he only has eyes for the woman. His synthesis of what she looks like may not be accurate, of course; somebody else may have a differing perception. We often say that someone is 'looking through the eyes of love' or that 'beauty is in the eye of

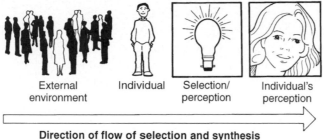

Direction of flow of selection and synthesis

Figure 4.4 Selection and synthesis in perception

the beholder'. These phrases accurately sum up what perception is all about.

From a marketing viewpoint, the fact that perception is so nebulous and individual a thing is probably helpful in the long run. People's views of products and services rely heavily on perceived attributes, some of which have no objective reality; the difficulty for marketers lies in knowing what will be the general perception of the members of the market segments with whom we are attempting to do business.

Key points from this chapter

This chapter has dealt with the processes which lead up to the formation of a view of the world. It has considered the main elements of learning and perception, and examined the arguments around classical and operant conditioning. Here are the main points again:

- Nearly all behaviour is learned.
- Learning may be automatic, without conscious thought (classical conditioning); or cognitive, where thought enters the equation.
- Learning is likely to rely to an extent on previous experience; knowledge is grouped into categories, or pigeonholes.
- Perception is both *analytic* and *synthetic*: information is selected out, then synthesized into a world-picture using elements taken from memory.
- The world-picture that results is incomplete, inaccurate and subjective.
- Minor, apparently irrelevant, stimuli can trigger an overall perception shift and result in positive or negative behaviour.

Notes

1. Sak Onkvisit and John J. Shaw, *Consumer Behaviour, Strategy and Analysis*, (New York: Macmillan, 1994).
2. Ivan P. Pavlov, *Conditioned Reflexes* (London: Oxford University Press, 1927).
3. Gerald J. Gorn, 'The effects of music in advertising on choice behaviour: a classical conditioning approach', *Journal of Marketing*, vol. 46 (Winter 1982), pp. 94–101.
4. Werner Kroeber-Riel, 'Emotional product differentiation by classical conditioning', in Thomas C. Kinnear (ed.), *Advances in Consumer Research*, vol. 11 (Provo, UT: Association for Consumer Research, 1984).
5. Frances K. McSweeney and Calvin Bierley, 'Recent developments in classical conditioning', *Journal of Consumer Research*, vol. 11 (Provo, UT: Association for Consumer Research, 1984).
6. Patrick Farrell, 'Sacred cows', *Marketing Business*, May 1996.
7. B.F. Skinner, *Science and Human Behaviour* (New York: Macmillan, 1953).
8. Stephen J. Hoch and Young-Won Ha, 'Consumer learning: advertising and the ambiguity of product experience', *Journal of Consumer Research*, vol. 13 (September 1986), pp. 221–33.
9. *Business Week*, 28 July 1980.
10. George A. Miller, 'The magical number seven, plus or minus two: some limits on our capacity for processing information', *Psychological Review* (March 1956), pp. 81–97.
11. Steuart Henderson Britt and Victoria M. Nelson, 'The marketing importance of the "just noticeable difference"', *Business Horizons*, vol. 14 (August 1976), pp. 38–40.
12. Steuart Henderson Britt, 'How Weber's Law can be applied to marketing', *Business Horizons*, vol. 13 (February 1975), pp. 21–9.

5

Attitudes

This chapter is about attitudes and how they are formed and changed. After reading this chapter, you should be able to:

- Explain how attitudes are formed.
- Describe the main theories on attitudes.
- Show how attitudes affect purchasing behaviour.
- Explain how attitude relates to action.
- Explain some of the ways in which attitudes can be changed.
- Describe the mechanisms of attitude change.

Introduction

Attitude can be defined as 'a learned tendency to respond to an object in a consistently favourable or unfavourable way'.[1] Whether a product will be bought or not depends to a large extent on the consumer's attitude towards it, and therefore much marketing effort is expended on finding out what consumers' attitudes are to product offerings, and seeking to change those attitudes where appropriate.

To break down the definition and make it easier to handle:

- Attitude is learned, not instinctive.
- It is not behaviour; it is a predisposition towards a particular behaviour.
- It implies a relationship between a person and an object. The object of the attitude could be another person, an institution or a physical article; 'object' is used here in the sense of 'an objective'.

- Attitudes are fairly stable; they do not change much with physical states or circumstances. For example, if a consumer's favourite painkiller is Panadol, that attitude remains whether or not the individual has a headache. The behaviour (actually taking the tablets) may not happen, but the attitude remains.
- The relationship between a person and an object is not neutral. It is a vector, having both direction and intensity. If you express an attitude about something, you either like it or you don't. If you are neutral about it, or indifferent, you would say you don't have any attitude towards it.

Attitude has to be inferred from statements or behaviour; it is intangible and not directly observable. In other words, although we can observe and measure behaviour, we have to ask people about their attitudes to various things, and hope that their replies are honest ones. This can cause difficulties if we are researching a sensitive topic.

The formation of attitude is based on *experience* with the object, normally from direct experience. Driving a particular make of car, or trying a particular brand of beer, will lead to the formation of an attitude. The individual builds up a mental picture (perception) of the object, and forms an attitude accordingly. First impressions are important, since they colour our later information gathering (see Chapter 4). This is why people behave themselves on the first date, so that the other person forms a favourable attitude.

Some experience is indirect; recommendations and the communicated experiences of friends or relatives are important when forming attitudes towards objects of which we don't have direct experience. This can sometimes lead to superstitious beliefs and prejudices due to the *synthetic* nature of perception. If your friends have all told you that a particular film is boring, you are likely to maintain that attitude, even if you have not seen the film yourself. Negative attitudes are often formed in this way. Advertising, and indeed marketing communications generally, can help a lot here by providing additional sources of information (public relations has a particularly important role in this, since it is an activity which deals mainly with attitude formation and change).

There is a perceptual component in attitude. The manner in which an object is perceived is affected by the consumer's stable characteristics (personality, intelligence, previous knowledge, culture, gender, etc.) and by current characteristics (mood, state of the organism, etc.).

Dimensions of attitude

Attitude has three dimensions, as Table 5.1 explains. It is important to note that attitude and behaviour are separate things. Simply because an

Table 5.1 Dimensions of attitude

Dimension	Definition	Explanation	Example
Cognition	The perceptual component of attitude	This is the individual's awareness, knowledge, beliefs and images of the attitudinal object. It is the conscious, thinking part of attitude.	An individual's attitude towards a car may be composed of comparative information, e.g. the Ford Escort has a tighter turning circle than the Vauxhall Cavalier, or the Vauxhall has better acceleration. These are the facts (or beliefs) informing the attitude.
Affect	The evaluative component of attitude	These are the emotions, the feelings of like and dislike which do not always have a basis in objective fact.	Drivers frequently have affective relationships with their first cars. The car is given a name, and often the driver will speak to it.
Conation	Behavioural intention	Conation is about what we intend to do about the attitudinal object: whether to approach it, reject it, buy it, etc. It is not the actual behaviour; merely an intention.	Having formed an attitude about a car ('I love the bodywork, it really looks great, and it does 40 to the gallon as well') the consumer forms an intention ('I'm going to take out a loan and buy one'). This intention is the conation.

individual has a particular attitude about something does not mean that the individual will act on the attitude. For example, you hear that your bank is investing in a country with an oppressive regime. This is *cognition*. You think that this is unethical, and you do not like the bank doing this (*affect*). You decide to move your account elsewhere (*conation*). Conation does not always lead to behaviour: you may have second thoughts later and decide to leave the account where it is, or something may prevent you from taking the course of action you had originally planned.

The three elements are interrelated in a complex way. Purchase intentions relate to beliefs and brand evaluations, and likelihood of buying a brand has been shown to be influenced by attitudes towards advertising as well as attitudes towards brands.[2]

The traditional view of attitude is that affect towards an object is *mediated* by cognition: in other words, emotional responses about something are controlled to a marked extent by rational evaluation. This has been challenged by Zajonc and Markus,[3] who assert that affective responses do not have to be based on prior cognition. People can develop a 'gut feel' about something without conscious evaluation, and even on limited information, then rationalize the decision afterwards. This may sometimes be due to classical conditioning: for example, the individual may form a favourable attitude towards a product because the advert uses a favourite song as background music (see Chapter 4).

Although it may seem illogical or dangerous to form an attitude without first finding out a lot about the attitudinal object, most people are familiar with the feeling of having 'fallen in love' with a hopelessly impractical purchase. Likewise, most people are familiar with the feeling of having taken an instant dislike to somebody without first getting to know the person.

Attitude contains components of belief and opinion, but it is neither. Attitude differs from *belief* in that belief is neutral, not implying good or bad. Belief is concerned with the presence or absence of an attribute, and is usually based on a judgement of the available evidence. Attitude contains an element of affect, and evaluates whether the existence of an attribute will result in satisfaction or dissatisfaction. For example, a consumer might believe that a Volvo is a reliable, well-engineered car, but have no particular feelings about this either way. Conversely, another consumer might feel that the Volvo is a good car, or a desirable car, because it is well engineered and reliable.

Attitude differs from *opinion* in that opinion is an overt, vocalized expression of an attitude. Attitude can also be expressed non-verbally (facial expressions, body language, etc.), or indeed may not be expressed at all. While opinions may arise from attitudes (i.e. be expressed as the result of an attitude) and attitudes may arise from hearing the opinions of others, the two are in fact separate entities.

Attitude formation

The formation of attitudes about brands is a somewhat complex process, as Figure 5.1 shows. The diagram begins with the consumer's needs, both utilitarian (practical) and expressive (emotional). This feeds into the consumer's motivation to process information, as does advertising; motivation and exposure feed into the processing, but the consumer also needs to have the ability and the opportunity to process the information.

Within the processing 'black box' the consumer's level of processing is affected by attention and capacity for processing: in other words, by the degree of interest the consumer has, and his or her ability to process the information. The result of the processing is both cognitive and affective, feeding into the formation of attitudes about the brand.

Situational variables surrounding the brand or product will also affect the attitude formation process. For example, an unpleasant salesperson or

ANTECEDENTS   PROCESSING   CONSEQUENCES

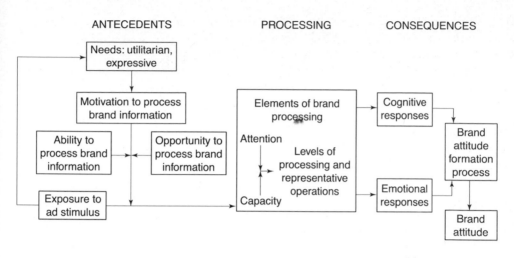

Figure 5.1 Formation of brand attitudes (Source: Deborah J. McInnis and Bernard J. Jaworski, 'Information processing from advertisements: toward an integrative framework', *Journal of Marketing*, vol. 53, October 1989, pp. 1–24)

an inconveniently located dealership may affect the way we perceive brands. Exposure to ad stimulus plays a major part in encouraging learning and the formation of attitudes, but the main drive comes (as always) from the consumer's needs.[4]

Consumers acquire *salient beliefs* about products. Because the cognitive system can hold only a relatively small number of facts in mind at once, the salient beliefs are the ones which are used by the consumer to make a judgement. Usually the salient beliefs will be those that the consumer holds most important, but they may be merely the ones that have been most recently presented.[5]

A consumer's overall attitude towards an object is a function of many attributes of the object. The attitude forms as a result of the consumer's strength of feeling, or the strength of the salient beliefs, about the attributes and also the evaluation of those beliefs. For example, a consumer may have the belief set about a restaurant given in Table 5.2. The question marks represent areas where the consumer has no knowledge, or has the knowledge but is not taking it into consideration. In other words, only the salient beliefs are taken into account.

This *multiattribute attitude model* attempts to explain how the consumer's salient beliefs help to form the final attitude. The attributes listed are integrated to form an overall attitude: in this example, the consumer will form an attitude about the restaurant as to whether it is a good restaurant or a bad one. The attitude may be qualified in some way – the restaurant may be regarded as a good one for lunch, but a bad one for dinner, or

Table 5.2 Example of a belief set

Attribute	Strength of salient belief (out of 10)	Level of importance (out of 10)
Convenient parking	5	7
Good food	6	8
Friendly waiters	?	4
Pleasant décor	7	5
Clean cutlery	3	7
Reasonable prices	?	3
Open on Wednesdays	?	5

perhaps as a good one for a quick meal when the consumer does not feel like cooking, but a bad one for special occasions.

Changing consumers' attitudes

The model is useful to marketers in that it helps when devising strategies for changing consumer attitudes. There are four ways of changing attitudes, as follows:

- *Add a new salient belief.* For example, the restaurant might point out that it has a strolling gypsy violinist on Saturday nights. This would be a new fact for the consumer to take into account.
- *Change the strength of a salient belief.* If the belief is a negative one, it can be discounted or played down; if it is a positive one, it can be given greater importance. In the above example, the consumer has a low level of belief in the cleanliness of the cutlery, but a high evaluation of this attribute. The restaurant should therefore make a point of telling customers that the cutlery is specially checked before it reaches the table.
- *Change the evaluation of an existing belief.* In the above example, the customer has a low evaluation of the price level in the restaurant: that is to say, the consumer is not really worried about getting a cheap meal. The restaurant could increase the evaluation of this attribute by pointing out that the low prices mean that the customer can come more often, or treat friends to a meal without breaking the bank.
- *Make an existing belief more salient.* In the example, the customer has indicated that the friendliness of the waiters is either not known or not salient. The restaurant could therefore emphasize that it makes a big difference to the enjoyment of the evening if the waiters are pleasant.

If the three components of attitude (cognition, affect and conation) are in balance, it is difficult to change the attitude because the attitude becomes stabilized. For example, if somebody is becoming overweight, believes that this is a bad thing, and therefore diets, the attitude is stable and would be difficult to change. If, on the other hand, the same person is overweight, believes that it is bad, but just somehow never gets round to dieting, it is relatively easy to tempt the person to 'treat' themselves to a snack or two.

Inconsistency between the three components of attitude will come about when a new stimulus is presented. New information might affect the cognitive or conative aspects, or a bad experience might change the affective aspects. When the degree of inconsistency between the three components exceeds a certain tolerance level, the individual will be compelled to undertake some kind of mental readjustment to restore stability. This can come about through three main defence mechanisms:

- Stimulus rejection.
- Attitude splitting.
- Accommodation to the new attitude.

Stimulus rejection means that the individual discounts the new information. For example, an overweight person might reject advice that slim people live longer than fat people, on the grounds that the research does not examine people who used to be fat but are now slim and have kept the weight off. By rejecting the new information, the individual is able to maintain the status quo as regards the cognitive element of attitude.

Attitude splitting involves accepting only that part of the information that does not cause an inconsistency. Here, the individual might accept that the new information is basically true, but that his or her own circumstances are exceptional. For example, if an individual finds out that the company he or she was planning to sue has gone bankrupt, this will alter the conative element of attitude, since it is impossible to sue a bankrupt company. The individual might agree that this is *generally* the case, but decide that the circumstances are such that he or she can sue the directors of the company instead.

Accommodation to the new attitude means, in effect, changing the attitude to accommodate the new information. The fat person may switch to a low-fat diet, the smoker may cut down or give up altogether, the prospective litigant may just chalk it up to experience.

The three elements are so closely related to each other that a change in one element will usually cause a change in the others.[6] New information causing a change in cognition will change the consumer's feelings about the product, which in turn is likely to change the consumer's intentions about the product.

The *elaboration likelihood model*[7] describes two routes by which attitude might be changed. The *central route* involves an appeal to the rational, cognitive element: the consumer makes a serious attempt to evaluate the new information in some logical way. The *peripheral route*, on the other hand, tends to involve the affective element by associating the product with another attitudinal object. For example, if a rock star appears in an ad for a soft drink, this might cause the star's fans to change their attitudes towards the drink. This has nothing to do with the attributes of the drink, but everything to do with the attributes of the star. Peripheral cues such as this are not relevant to a reasoned evaluation, but because of the interdependence of the components of attitude, change will occur. In effect, the affect felt towards the star 'rubs off' on the product.

Changing existing attitudes relies heavily on market research, but the teasing out of the factors which go to make up the attitude can be a particularly demanding task. This is because of *halo effect*. Halo effect is the tendency for attitudes about one salient belief to colour attitudes about another. For example, if a consumer had a bad meal at a restaurant, this is likely to lead to a view that everything else about the restaurant was bad, too. Likewise a favourable view of some factors often leads to respondents reporting a favourable view of other factors.

Attitude measurement

Measuring attitudes is clearly a subject of some interest to marketers, since attitudes play such a major role in consumer purchasing behaviour. It is obviously of importance for manufacturers to know what the consumers' attitude is to the product, but it is difficult to quantify. This is because attitude contains elements of both cognition and affect. Here are two contrasting models for attitude measurement: the Rosenberg model and the Fishbein model.

The *Rosenberg model*[8] says that an individual's attitude towards an object represents the degree and direction of the attitudinal effect aroused by the object. Put more simply, attitude is composed of a *quantity* of feeling and a *direction*, and has two main components:

- *Perceived instrumentality.* This is the subjective capacity of the object to attain the value in question: in other words, the usefulness of the object.
- *Value importance.* This is the amount of satisfaction the person derives from the attainment of a particular value. More simply, it is the importance of achieving the result that the consumer is hoping to achieve by buying and using the object of the attitude.

Perceived instrumentality means the degree to which the consumer thinks the product will work as it is supposed to. Value importance is the degree to which getting the job done is important to the consumer.

Theoretically, perceived instrumentality and value importance are actually independent, and taken separately they do not predict responses well, but taken together they are good predictors of behaviour that is illustrative of attitude.

The *Fishbein model*[9] takes a different perspective on the problem, by focusing on the consumer rather than on the product. For Fishbein, attitudes can be predicted from beliefs and evaluation. Belief is the probability that the object possesses a particular attribute; evaluation is whether that attribute attracts or repels. This is not compatible with the value importance concept in the Rosenberg model.

In this model, the consumer's belief in the product's capabilities replaces the perceived instrumentality aspect. For example, it may be useful for a car to have a large boot (Rosenberg model), but whether a particular car's boot is large or not is a relative term and relies on the consumer's beliefs (Fishbein model). Furthermore, the belief that a car's boot is large does not necessarily mean that the prospective owner will like that attribute (Fishbein model). This will depend on how important the attribute is to the customer (Rosenberg model).

Combining the two models, there are three distinct aspects of attitude:

- Perceived instrumentality.
- Evaluative aspect (affect).
- Value importance.

Examples of these aspects are as follows:

- I believe the Vauxhall Cavalier is the most comfortable car in its class.
- I like comfort.
- Comfort is very important to me.

Note that the second two are not identical. You can like something without it being very important to you.

Functions of attitudes

Attitudes have a function in helping consumers make decisions about their purchasing practices, and also serve other functions according to the individual's circumstances. Four main categories of function have been identified, as shown in Table 5.3.[10]

Table 5.3 Functions of attitude

Function	Definition	Explanation	Example
Instrumental function	The individual uses the attitude to obtain satisfaction from the object.	The individual thus aims to maximize external reward while minimizing external punishment.	An individual might develop an attitude towards a particular pub because his friends go there and the beer is good.
Ego-defensive function	Protects against internal conflicts and external dangers.	Here the attitude shields the individual from his/her own failings.	A rioter blaming the police for his injuries.
Value-expressive function	Opposite of ego-defensive; the drive for self-expression.	The attitudes expressed often go against the flow of opinion.	Most radical political viewpoints are examples of the value-expressive attitude in action.
Knowledge function	The drive to seek clarity and order.	Related to the need to understand what the object is all about. Comes from the belief that if you know what you like and dislike, decision making is easy.	Somebody who has an interest in hi-fi systems is likely to read magazines about them, to visit exhibitions and to discuss them with friends so as to know what the latest products are.

Attitude and behaviour

The *theory of reasoned action*[11] says that consumers consciously evaluate the consequences of alternative behaviours, and then choose the one that will lead to the most favourable consequences. Figure 5.2 shows the four main components of the theory: behaviour, intention to behave, attitude towards the behaviour, and subjective norm. The subjective norm is the component which reflects the social pressures that the individual may feel to perform (or avoid performing) the behaviour being contemplated.

The individual's beliefs about the behaviour and the evaluation of the possible main consequences will combine to produce an attitude about the behaviour. At the same time, the individual's beliefs about what other people might think, and the degree to which he or she cares about what other people think, go towards developing a subjective norm about the contemplated behaviour. The individual will then weight the relative importance of the attitude and the norm, and will form an intention of how to behave. This may, in turn, lead to the behaviour itself.

The theory of reasoned action assumes that consumers perform a logical evaluation procedure for making decisions about behaviour, based on

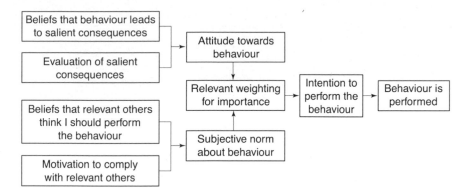

Figure 5.2 The theory of reasoned action (Source: Martin Fishbein, 'An overview of the attitude construct', in G.B. Hafer (ed.), *A Look Back, A Look Ahead*, Chicago, IL: American Marketing Association, 1980)

attitude towards the behaviour, which in turn derives from attitudes towards the product or brand.

Logically, attitude should precede behaviour. In other words, we would expect the consumer to form an attitude about something, then to act on that attitude. In fact, much of the evidence points the other way. It appears in some cases that people behave first, and form attitudes afterwards.[12]

Marketing efforts often encourage people to buy first, then form attitudes: free samples, test drives, demonstrations and coupons are all more powerful in forming attitude and behaviour consistency than are advertisements.[13] Attitudes formed without trial experience are probably weak and easily changed. In this context, the Pepsi Challenge represents a way of persuading people that Pepsi is better than Coca-Cola. Each summer, stands are set up in shopping malls and at seaside resorts, and passers-by are offered the chance to compare Pepsi with Coca-Cola in a blind taste test. People are frequently surprised to find that they actually prefer the Pepsi.

Part of the reason for this is that the two drinks do, in fact, taste very similar, and without the visual cue of the packaging, the consumers often cannot tell the difference between the two. Since Pepsi has a smaller market share than Coca-Cola, the company only needs half of the respondents to prefer the Pepsi in order to gain a greater market share than it currently holds.

Trial of a product is so much more powerful than advertising in forming favourable impressions that car manufacturers are prepared to give special deals to car rental companies and driving schools in order to encourage hirers and learners to buy the same model at a later date.

It may not matter greatly whether attitude precedes behaviour or not. Attitude is not always followed by the proposed behaviour; most people are familiar with having proposed doing something, then having done

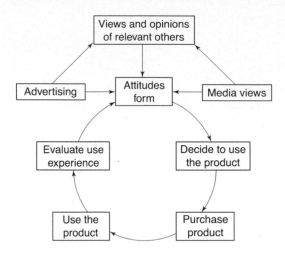

Figure 5.3 Cycle of attitude and behaviour

something else instead. This may be because attitude and behaviour are not always consistent. For example, a smoker may take the attitude that smoking is unhealthy and antisocial, but may still not give up smoking. Dieting is a similar example: even though a fat person may believe that being fat is unhealthy and unattractive, losing weight may not be the end result. In Freudian terms, the attitude may have come from the superego, but the demands of the id result in a failure to act.

In fact, it seems more likely that, at least regarding fast-moving consumer goods (FMCG), the processes of attitude formation and behaviour are interwoven. Figure 5.3 illustrates this. In this model, there is a feedback loop that allows the consumer to re-evaluate and reconsider his or her attitudes. The formation of attitude is thus seen as a dynamic process, with the behaviour itself forming part of the process.

Private versus public attitudes

People often hold attitudes that they are reluctant to admit to in public. This is particularly true in recent years due to the fashion for political correctness. This makes attitude measurement difficult because respondents will give a rational or acceptable answer rather than a true one: few people would be prepared to admit openly that they have racist attitudes, for example, yet it is undoubtedly the case that many people do have such attitudes.

In marketing terms, people are often reluctant to admit to buying products which are embarrassing (or illegal). Most people would be reluctant to admit, for instance, that they like pornography, and therefore it is easier to sell such products through the post than it is to sell them through retail outlets. Mail order preserves the anonymity of the customer.

Clearly there are implications for market research, since any questions which enquire into these attitudes are likely to meet with evasive answers or just plain lies. Most people will have some private attitudes and some opposing public attitudes, and therefore measurement of these private attitudes can best be carried by using *projective* techniques such as *sentence completion* or *cartoon tests*. In a sentence completion test, the respondent is asked to complete a sentence such as 'I think people who buy pornography are . . . .' In a cartoon test, the subject is asked to fill in the speech bubbles on a cartoon picture of somebody in a purchasing situation. In theory, the subject will state what he or she would say in that situation, but is not put in the (embarrassing) position of actually having to express the opinion first-hand.

People's private attitudes often do not have a logical basis, and therefore the individuals concerned are even more reluctant to admit to holding these views. Sometimes there is a reluctance to express an opinion when it has no logical basis; attitude, as we have seen, has a strong affective component.

Attitude versus situation

During the 1930s, in a hotel in the south of France, a strange ceremony was acted out daily. One of the Romanov princes (from the Russian royal family) would ask his chauffeur to mash up a plate of strawberries and then eat them. This ceremony took place every day, even when the strawberries had to be specially flown in for the purpose. The reason was that the prince loved the smell of strawberries, but was allergic to them and therefore could not eat them. His attitude towards the 'product' therefore could not result in his consuming it, due to his situation.

Positive attitude towards the product may not equate to positive attitude about the *purchase* of the product. A consumer may have a strong positive attitude towards light-coloured clothes, but not buy them because she works in the city and light-coloured clothes show the dirt.

Fishbein suggests that the model be modified to take account of this.[14] The attitude to be measured should, under the extended model, be the attitude towards performing a given act (e.g. purchase or consumption) rather than an attitude towards the object itself. The evidence is that this model is a better predictor of purchasing behaviour than merely measuring attitudes towards the brands themselves, but of course there is greater complexity involved in understanding why a consumer has a particular attitude, since more variables are involved.

Attitudes can be changed due to situational changes. For example, a sudden drop in disposable income might lead somebody to think that a product is too expensive, even if it was seen as good value for money previously. Intentions can be checked against later performance by means of garbage analysis or self-report: Cote, McCullough and Reilly found that 'behaviour–intention inconsistency is partly attributable to unexpected situations'.[15]

Attitude towards ads versus attitude towards the brand

An individual may love the ads and hate the product, or vice versa. Although there is an assumption that a positive attitude towards the advertisement will lead to a positive attitude about the product, the two are actually separate hypothetical constructs.[16] This is because the attitude towards the brand is affected by many more factors than the advertisement, whereas attitude towards the advertisement is affected only by the ad itself. The perception of the brand is much more likely to have a major cognitive element in it, whereas most advertising is intended to produce an affective response.

General versus specific attitudes

It is necessary to look at specific attitudes when attempting to predict behaviour. It is possible to hold one attitude generally, but an opposing attitude in a specific case: for example, it is possible to dislike children while still loving one's own children, or to like wine in general but to dislike Lambrusco. For marketers, the important attitude to measure is, of course, the attitude to the specific brand rather than the attitude to the product class as a whole.

Having said that, there is an issue regarding brand switching. If a consumer has a generally negative attitude about a product class, but will use a specific brand within that class, it may be possible to switch the consumer towards another brand which is similar to the one that is already acceptable. Consumers may already be prepared to do this in the event that the desired brand is out of stock; the difficulty lies in knowing why the individual consumer has made the decision to keep to only one brand of a class of products that he or she dislikes.

For example, a consumer may feel that, generally speaking, mayonnaise is thoroughly disgusting, with the exception of Hellman's. It is possible that the consumer could be switched to Heinz if the Hellmann's is out of stock, but this would happen only if the consumer could be persuaded that the Heinz is just as good. If it turns out that the consumer is allergic to every other brand but Hellmann's, however, there will not be any way of achieving a brand switch.

Key points from this chapter

In this chapter we have looked at attitudes and how they are formed and maintained. We have also looked at ways of changing attitudes, and at some of the theories of attitude measurement. The key points from the chapter are as follows:

- Attitude is a learned construct which shows a person's tendency to respond to an object in a consistently favourable or unfavourable manner.
- Attitude is not neutral.
- Although attitude is not behaviour, it can be inferred from behaviour.
- Likewise, behaviour can be inferred from attitude, but the relationship is not reliable.
- Attitude is multidimensional, comprising affect, cognition and conation.
- Consumers only use salient beliefs when forming attitudes, not all the facts.
- Attitudes serve four useful purposes: instrumental, ego-defensive, value expressive and knowledge.
- Behaviour affects attitude more than attitude affects behaviour (see Burris Skinner).

Notes

1. Sak Onkvisit and John J. Shaw, *Consumer Behaviour, Strategy and Analysis* (New York: Macmillan, 1994).
2. Pamela M. Homer and Sun-Gil Yoon, 'Message framing and the interrelationships among ad-based feelings, affect and cognition', *Journal of Advertising*, vol. 21 (March 1992), pp. 19–33.
3. Robert B. Zajonc and Hazel Markus, 'Must all affect be mediated by cognition?', *Journal of Consumer Research*, vol. 12 (December 1985), pp. 363–4.
4. Ida E. Berger and Andrew A. Mitchell, 'The effect of advertising on attitude accessibility, attitude confidence, and the attitude–behaviour relationship', *Journal of Consumer Research*, vol. 16 (December 1989), pp. 269–79.

5. Martin Fishbein and Icek Ajzen, *Belief, Attitude, Intention and Behaviour: An introduction to theory and research* (Reading, MA: Addison-Wesley, 1975).
6. Milton J. Rosenberg, 'An analysis of affective-cognitive consistency', in Milton J. Rosenberg *et al.* (eds.), *Attitude Organisation and Change* (New Haven, CT: Yale University Press, 1960).
7. Richard E. Petty and John T. Cacioppo, 'Central and peripheral routes to persuasion: application to advertising', in Larry Percy and Arch Woodside (eds.), *Advertising and Consumer Psychology* (Lexington, MA: Lexington Books, 1983).
8. Milton J. Rosenberg, 'Inconsistency arousal and reduction in attitude change', *Public Opinion Quarterly*, vol. 24 (1960), pp. 319–40.
9. Martin Fishbein, 'An overview of the attitude construct', in G.B. Hafer (ed.), *A Look Back, A Look Ahead* (Chicago, IL: American Marketing Association, 1980).
10. William B. Locander and W. Austin Spivey, 'A functional approach to the study of attitude measurement', *Journal of Marketing Research*, vol. 15 (November 1978), pp. 576–87.
11. Icek Ajzen and Martin Fishbein, *Understanding Attitudes and Predicting Social Behaviour* (Englewood Cliffs, NJ: Prentice Hall 1980).
12. Martin Fishbein, 'The search for attitudinal–behavioural consistency', in Joel E. Cohen (ed.), *Behavioural Science Foundations of Consumer Behaviour* (New York: Free Press, 1972).
13. Robert E. Smith and William R. Swinyard, 'Attitude–behaviour consistency: the impact of product trial versus advertising', *Journal of Marketing Research*, vol. 20 (August 1983).
14. Fishbein, 'Attitudinal–behavioural consistency', *op. cit.*
15. Joseph A. Cote, James McCullough and Michael Reilly, 'Effects of unexpected situations on behaviour–intention differences: a garbology analysis', *Journal of Consumer Research*, vol. 15 (December 1988), pp. 188–94.
16. Andrew A. Mitchell, 'The effect of verbal and visual components of advertisements on brand attitudes and attitudes towards the advertisements', *Journal of Consumer Research*, vol. 13 (June 1986), pp. 12–24.

6

The environment, class and culture

This chapter is about the influences surrounding consumers in their everyday decision-making situations. It describes some of the forces that mould consumer thinking, and some of the main factors in the consumer's environment.

After reading this chapter, you should be able to:

- Describe how the decision-making environment can affect consumer behaviour.
- Explain the main concepts surrounding class and culture.
- Explain how cultural factors can affect decision-making processes.

The environment: situational influences

Behaviour always occurs within a situation, or context; situational influence arises from factors which are independent of either the consumer or the object (product) of the purchase behaviour.[1] Situational influences involve both people and objects, and the influences that are inherent in the situation itself.

Situational influences can be defined along five dimensions: physical surroundings, social surroundings, time, task and antecedent states.[2]

Physical surroundings might include geographical location, décor, sounds, smells, lighting, weather and the layout of the product displays surrounding the product. The physical surroundings affect the mood of the individual, and therefore will colour the individual's attitude towards the product. For example, some supermarkets use aerosol sprays with the aroma of fresh-baked bread in order to give an impression of warmth and security, and to increase the sales of bread in the store. Décor in retail outlets is often designed to be relaxing, so that the shoppers will stay longer and perhaps buy more. Some stores use calming music for the same reason, although this has declined in recent years in UK supermarkets because shoppers sometimes found the music irritatingly bland.

Social surroundings concern the presence (or absence) of other people in the situation. The *macro* social environment refers to the interactions between very large groups of people, and (broadly speaking) divides into three areas: culture, subculture and social class. The *micro* social environment is concerned with the more intimate, face-to-face interactions between friends, family members and reference groups. There is more on this in Chapter 7. At the macro level, marketers might be concerned with mass advertising and large-scale campaigns; at the micro level, marketing would be concerned with personal selling or multilevel marketing systems.

Time is concerned with the moment the behaviour occurs. This could relate to the time of day, the day of the week, the season, or the relative time since the last (or next) purchase. Much consumption is geared to *time of day*: for example, most people have a clear idea of what constitutes suitable breakfast food, and will often have the same thing for breakfast every day, even though this judgement may change from one country to another. The traditional British fried breakfast would seem very unsuitable to a Frenchman who is used to coffee and croissants, and a Sri Lankan breakfast of crisp rice-flour pancakes and curry sauces might seem unsuitable to British people.

Likewise the *season of the year* dictates purchasing behaviour: sales of sausages, burgers and spare ribs rise during the summer when people are enjoying barbecues. The *day of the week* affects purchases of hairdressing, nights out, and takeaway foods, which all have increased sales on Fridays and Saturdays. *Elapsed time* since the last purchase affects car sales, food sales and TV licence purchase.

Task comprises the particular goals and objectives that the consumer has at the time. For example, buying Christmas presents for the family involves a completely different approach from buying items for the consumer's own use. Buying a car with the objective of impressing the neighbours (or clients) will lead to a different solution from that of buying a car to go on safari to Cape Town.

The *antecedent state* is the temporary mood or condition that the consumer brings to the situation: tiredness, excitement, lack of cash, or perhaps a new purchase which needs an accessory. Antecedent states need to be distinguished from states that occur in response to the purchasing situation, for example as the result of an interrupt or a change in the heuristic; 'antecedent' actually means pre-existing. Antecedent states should also be distinguished from personality in that they are temporary. They do exert considerable influence on buying behaviour: somebody who is running short of money will often spend much more time considering purchases than will somebody with plenty of cash on hand, or alternatively somebody who is in an excited state might well be more reckless with money and make rapid, impulsive decisions.

These five characteristics of situations come into play in different ways according to the type of situation the consumer is faced with. In *information acquisition* or *communications* situations, the consumer is sometimes overloaded with information and finds it difficult to sort out the wheat from the chaff. For example, TV advertising typically comes in three-minute breaks which contain between six and eight advertising messages. Since the messages are usually intense, stimulating bursts of information, the TV viewer finds it difficult to ignore them without actually turning off the sound or leaving the room, but at the same time the amount of information contained cannot be taken in all at once. Likewise, magazine advertising is so intense that the reader cannot possibly read all the ads, and therefore skips pages with ads on. This is called *advertising clutter* and is a growing problem for marketers,[3] since it results in ever-increasing rejection of advertising by consumers. Typically, people will use the advertising breaks to make a cup of tea, go to the toilet, make a telephone call, or otherwise avoid the message. TV remote controls are used to turn off the sound, or the ad breaks are clipped out of video recordings so that the programme can be watched uninterrupted.

Communications situations often involve a dilemma for consumers, in that their desire for information is moderated by a fear of being 'sold to'. In other words, even though the advertisement might be of interest, or the salesperson might be worth talking to, the consumer may avoid the situation rather than risk information overload, or being inveigled into something.

Shopping situations refer to the retail environment. This can range from a pedestrianized shopping street to a suburban High Street, or a shopping centre to an out-of-town retail park. Each has its own atmosphere and characteristics, and each will generate specific consumer behaviour. For example, out-of-town retail parks will mainly attract car drivers, since the public transport accessibility is usually limited. This means that such retail parks are predominantly used for major shopping trips, either to make major purchases of consumer durables or to buy the weekly grocery shopping. Shopping behaviour will be different in a shopping centre from behaviour in a street market, and in each case the consumer's expectations of price, quality, and service will be different.

Purchasing situations refer to the retail environment within the shops themselves. The factors included in the purchasing situation range from the social (the attitude of the shop assistants) to the physical (the décor and layout of the shop). *Store atmospherics* are particularly important in this respect, and since most of the situational aspects of consumption are

Table 6.1 Effects of store atmospherics

Effect of atmospherics	Explanation
Shape the direction and duration of consumers' attention	If the customer stays in the shop longer, this is likely to lead to greater *product contact*. This, in turn, might lead to the customer buying something extra.
Express various aspects of the shop to its customers	A shop with a cheap décor and basic displays portrays a low-price image; a shop with luxurious décor and artful displays portrays a high-quality image.
Convey emotions such as pleasure and interest	If the consumer is enjoying the shop, he or she is likely to spend more time (and money) in it.

Sources: Philip J. Kotler, 'Atmospherics as a marketing tool', *Journal of Retailing*, vol. 49 (Winter 1973–4), pp. 48–64; Robert J. Donovan and John R. Rossiter, 'Store atmosphere: an environmental psychology approach', *Journal of Retailing*, vol. 58 (Spring 1982), p. 42.

beyond the marketers' control, much attention is paid to store atmospherics, which can be controlled by the marketer. The general *ambience* within each shop will affect the consumer's perception of the store.

For example, discount stores such as KwikSave and Aldi deliberately use cheap décor, basic displays and rather Spartan surroundings because this conveys the impression that the goods are therefore cheaper than they would be in more expensively fitted shops. At the other end of the scale, the upmarket fashion houses provide their customers with wine and coffee while the clothes are modelled for them in luxurious surroundings. The effects of store atmospherics on customers are shown in Table 6.1.

When designing the store interior, the managers will take into account the shopping situation. An edge-of-town Tesco superstore will have wider checkout aisles, more trolleys and fewer baskets, and a greater range of bulky items than will a Tesco Metro store. This is because the edge-of-town superstore is mainly used by people who are doing their main weekly shopping, and predominantly by people who have driven to the store and can therefore easily carry bulky items, whereas the Metro store is geared towards the lunchtime, after-work and local shoppers, who will probably arrive on foot or by bus and will have to carry the shopping home. Hence the quantities purchased will be correspondingly less than in the superstore.

Other factors in the retail environment are music, layout and colours. *Music* has become largely obsolete in UK stores due to negative customer responses (although it is still utilized in some purchasing situations, such as restaurants). The *layout* of the shop is often crucial to its success. Sugar, which shows a low profit margin, is often placed at the far end of the store so as to maximize *product contact* as customers search for it. Confectionery and impulse-type goods are often placed near checkouts, new products are placed in high-traffic areas, and traffic flows are designed to ensure that shoppers will be directed past sensitive areas.

Colours affect consumers' perceptions and behaviour in a subtle way. Warm colours such as yellow and red are more attractive, whereas cool colours are more relaxing but are also less attractive. Research has shown that warm colours are more suitable for the outsides of shops (so that customers are attracted in) and cool colours such as blues and greens are more suitable for the insides of shops, so that consumers are encouraged to remain within the shop, thus increasing the chances of product contact.[4]

Included within the purchasing situation are funds access and the final transaction. Both these areas are crucial for the marketer to control; retailers will try to ensure that the customer can access sufficient money to make the purchase. For this reason, most shops will accept credit cards. A useful spin-off for retailers from this policy is that the stores do not have as much cash on the premises at the end of the working day, so that security costs are also lower. Major out-of-town retail parks also have cash points; the aim is to ensure that the customer is never short of the wherewithal to pay for the goods.

Consumption situations surround the actual use or consumption of the products. In most cases, marketers have no direct control over the consumption situation, and can only make suggestions through advertising. An example of this is After Eight Mints, which virtually single-handedly invented the idea of an after-dinner chocolate. For some products, the consumption behaviour may take place over a long period (for example, consumption of a microwave oven may take ten years or more).

On the other hand, products with a high service content may allow marketers to control the consumption environment better. Brewers are able to control pub environments with a considerable degree of accuracy; and for purely service-orientated products such as hairdressing or health-care services, the product is delivered entirely within a controlled environment.

Disposition situations are of increasing interest to marketers. These are the situations under which consumers dispose of the used-up and unwanted products. In some cases these products are simply thrown away, but in others the consumer gives the product to a charity shop, sells it at a car-boot sale, or trades it in for a newer model. In each case the marketer has an interest.

In the case of discarded products, many marketers now feel obligated to ensure that the product will not pollute the environment or represent a health hazard. For example, fast-food outlets are under considerable pressure to ensure that uneaten food and soiled packaging are not simply left in the surrounding environment; in the case of McDonald's this has led to the establishment of clean-up squads who patrol the immediate area around the restaurant collecting litter. In the case of charity-shop gifts and car-boot sales, marketers may find that the market for new products is damaged somewhat by the presence of these (cheaper) alternatives.

One response that has been widely adopted is the trade-in discount. Originally developed in the 1930s by General Motors executives, the trade-in has become a fixed feature of the motor trade. The existence of trade-in has ensured that there is a steady market for new cars, and the second-hand car trade remains largely under the control of the major manufacturers in the car industry, since they set the trade-in values against new cars. From time to time similar trade-in discounts have been introduced in markets for other consumer durables, but since the second-hand market for most consumer durables is less well developed, such discounts have been seen mainly as sales promotion ploys rather than as major contributors to the marketing of new products.

The *person–situation interface* refers to the synergy between the person and the situation. Not everybody responds in the same way to a given situation: for example, although most people tend to spend more on groceries when it is a long time since their last meal, overweight people do not do so to the same extent.[5] It has even been argued that markets should be segmented not only by type of consumer, but also according to the situation in which the product is to be bought, used or disposed of.[6]

Situations can change, and in so doing can change the consumer's buying intentions. For example, a change in the décor of a restaurant can prompt a diner to eat elsewhere, or the closing-down of a recycling scheme might cause a consumer to buy products with different packaging. These situational changes can lose customers or gain them; most marketers hope that the gains and losses will balance out, but this is not necessarily the case.

Culture

Culture is a set of beliefs and values that are shared by most people within a group. The groupings considered under culture are usually relatively large, but at least in theory a culture can be shared by a few people. Culture is passed on from one group member to another, and in particular is usually passed down from one generation to the next; it is learned, and is therefore both *subjective* and *arbitrary*.

For example, food is strongly linked to culture. While cheese is regarded as a delicacy in France, and the country boasts several hundred different varieties, in Japan cheese is regarded as being as appealing as rotted milk and is rarely eaten. Likewise, few British people would be prepared to eat insects, yet regard prawns as a treat; orthodox Jews would not eat prawns at all, since shellfish are not kosher. These differences in tastes are explained by the culture rather than by some random differences in taste between

Table 6.2 Examples of fundamental cultural variations

Aspect	Description	Explanation
Time	Attitudes towards time can divide into two main approaches: the traditional view of time, and the modern view. The traditional view holds that each day will be replaced by a new day tomorrow, and that therefore it does not greatly matter if a day is wasted, since what is not done today can just as easily be done tomorrow. The modern view holds that each day is unique, will never come again and should therefore not be wasted.	The traditional view is more common in agricultural societies. Typical of hot countries where the day and seasons do not vary much, it is typified by the 'mañana' approach. In such countries, appointments may not be kept and queues may be long – after all, what is there to rush for, when there will be another day tomorrow? In Europe and North America, however, there is pressure to achieve the maximum from each passing minute and therefore people would resent being kept waiting.
Space	There are two categories of consideration about space: first, the concept of personal space (the amount of space a person prefers to have around him/her); and second, the use of space in the surrounding environment.	Typically, British and American people tend to keep their distance from strangers, and prefer not to be in close proximity to other people. This is in contrast with Middle Eastern people, who prefer to be close to anybody with whom they are having a discussion.

individuals; the behaviours are shared by people from a particular cultural background.

Language is also particularly culturally based. Even when a language is shared across cultures, there will be differences according to the local culture; differences between American English and British English are well known, but there are even differences between Lancashire English and Newcastle English. The potential for misunderstandings is great, and since each person imagines that the other understands the cultural context as well as the language, any discrepancies tend to be attributed to stupidity or malice on the part of the other person.

Most cultures have as one of their characteristics the idea of *ethnocentrism*: the belief that their own culture is the 'right' one and everybody else's culture is at best a poor imitation, at worst an evil travesty. Some examples of cultural differences in some fundamental aspects of daily life are given in Table 6.2.

Because culture is a shared set of beliefs, it is not surprising that national cultural characteristics can sometimes be identified. Hofstede[7] carried out a transnational survey in 66 countries, with over 6,000 respondents. He was able to identify four dimensions of national characteristics, as follows:

- *Individualism versus collectivism.* Some cultures value individualism and individual freedom more highly than collectivism and service to the group. The US and Holland show strong individualistic tendencies, whereas Far Eastern countries such as Taiwan and Japan show collectivist tendencies. Individualism is on the increase in the UK (in common with most industrialized countries) and this has been particularly strongly identified with the Generation X group (those born in the late 1960s and 1970s).[8]

- *Uncertainty avoidance.* This refers to the degree to which the people of the country keep to rules and customs in order to reduce uncertainty. A high level of uncertainty avoidance would indicate a culture where traditional values prevail, and where new ideas or unusual lifestyles would not be tolerated. A low level of uncertainty avoidance implies a culture where people tend to be tolerant of new ideas, and consequently are likely to change the culture.

- *Power distance.* This refers to the degree to which the culture favours the centralization of power, and the extent to which people from different levels in the power hierarchy are able to have contact with one another. Power distance also affects the acceptance of earning differentials and wealth concentration: countries like Brazil and India have high wealth concentrations (i.e. a high proportion of the country's wealth is concentrated in the hands of a few people), whereas countries like Holland and Belgium have low wealth concentrations.

- *Masculinity–femininity.* This refers to the degree to which the culture exhibits the traditional masculine characteristics of assertiveness, achievement and wealth acquisition rather than the traditional feminine attributes of nurturing, concern for the environment and concern for the poor. The USA, for example, is a strongly masculine culture.

While cultural generalities such as these are interesting and useful, it would be dangerous to make assumptions about individuals from other countries based on the kind of general findings in Hofstede's work. Individuals from within a culture differ more than do the cultures from each other: in other words, the most individualistic Taiwanese is a great deal more individualistic than the most conformist American. Having said that, such generalizations are useful when approaching mass markets, and are certainly widely used when planning mass advertising campaigns such as TV commercials.

Advertising is often deeply rooted in the local culture, and therefore cannot often be transferred across national boundaries; advertisements transfer cultural meaning into products.[9] Advertisements often use *symbols* which might be meaningless to members of a different culture: for example, a British ad might use a lion to symbolize patriotism, whereas an American ad would use a bald eagle and a French ad might use a cockerel. Likewise, verbal cues will differ, even when the language used is (ostensibly) the same. This is because of the use of slang, and also because of differing literary references across cultures. Catchphrases derived from TV shows will differ between the USA and the UK: few Americans would recognize catchphrases from *One Foot in the Grave*, and few Brits would recognize catchphrases from *All in the Family*.

Because of these cultural differences, advertising and branding differ across national boundaries. The Nescafé Gold Blend ads are run in the USA, the UK and Denmark, but the Danes are about two years behind in the plot and the brand is called Oro; the Americans are some four years behind and the brand is Taster's Choice. The ads are dubbed into the appropriate language. The Werther's Original ads are reshot so that the grandfather and grandson are more culturally acceptable in each region, but the basic plot of the ads remains the same. Some brand names have to be changed to meet local language problems: famous examples include the Vauxhall Nova ('no va' in Spanish meaning 'doesn't go') and Irish Mist liqueur ('mist' meaning 'dung' in German). More subtly, advertisements produced for one culture often seem irritating or laughable in another culture.

Subculture refers to a set of beliefs shared by a subgroup of the main culture. Although this subgroup will share most of the beliefs of the main culture, they share among themselves another set of beliefs which may be at odds with those held by the main group. For example, skinheads may share the mainstream British culture in terms of watching TV, drinking beer, living in houses, speaking English and so forth, but have a distinct subculture of wearing boots and braces and having cropped hair. This expresses at a formal level the 'hardness, masculinity and working-classness' of the group's situation and experiences.[10]

The adoption of spectacular forms of dress (such as boots and braces, or the punk style, or the earlier adoption of zoot suits) is a way of proclaiming cultural identity and showing that the wearer is a member of a specific group. Likewise, adaptations of other cultural elements (for example, language) accumulate to become a specific *style*.[11]

Culture can change over a period of time, although such changes tend to be slow, since culture is deeply built into people's behaviour. From a marketing viewpoint, therefore, it is probably much easier to work within a given culture than to try to change it.

Class

Some sociologists regard class as being one of the central issues of the discipline, yet it is an ill-defined and ambiguous concept.[12] For the lay-person, social class is beginning to seem like an outmoded concept: the old class distinctions appear to be breaking down as machines replace heavy physical labour, and even the aristocracy now work for a living.

Table 6.3 Classification of socioeconomic groups

Social grade	Social status	Head of household's occupation	Approx. percentage of families
A	Upper middle class	Higher managerial, administrative or professional	3
B	Middle class	Intermediate managerial, administrative or professional	10
C1	Lower middle class	Supervisory or clerical, and junior managerial, administrative or professional	24
C2	Skilled working class	Skilled manual workers	30
D	Working class	Semi- and unskilled manual workers	25
E	Those at lowest levels of subsistence	State pensioners or widows (no other earner), casual or lowest-grade workers	8

Social class is predominantly defined by the occupation of the individual.[13] Individuals may then be grouped into classifications such as skilled manual, unskilled manual, higher managerial and professional, and so forth. In recent years the process has become complicated by the fact that the majority of married women now work outside the home, leading to a debate among sociologists as to whether these women should be categorized according to their partner's occupation, or according to their own.[14]

Table 6.3 shows the classification of socioeconomic groups. Although this classification is still widely used, it should be used with some caution, since its relevance to an individual's buying behaviour is now somewhat limited.

There is, of course, more to social class than occupation. Class also implies a position in the power hierarchy: the further up the class ladder an individual is, the more power and influence he or she has. This can vary from the small powers of discretion exercised by a factory foreman up to the hire-and-fire decisions exercised by a managing director. This gradual increase of power and discretion towards the top of the social order has marketing implications. For example, Karl Marx said that 'The ideas of the ruling class are, in every age, the ruling ideas', and this thinking has led to the *trickle-down theory* of diffusion of innovation (see Chapter 8). Table 6.4 shows the relationship between social class, role in the capitalist structure, and type of occupation.

Max Weber defined class in terms of life chances.[15] A class is a group of people who have in common a specific causal component of their life chances which is represented by possession of goods and opportunities for income, and which operates under the conditions of the commodity or

Table 6.4 Production, class and occupation

Social relations of production	Class structure	Occupational categories
Functions of capital relating to:		
Ownership	Middle class	Shareholders and proprietors
Control and co-ordination		Directors, managers, higher-grade professional employees
Research and technological development		Scientists, engineers and technologists
Functions of labour relating to:		
Production of economic surplus	Working class	Productive manual workers
Execution of necessary but non-productive tasks		Clerical, secretarial, routine non-manual, support and maintenance workers

Source: Richard Scase, *Class* (Buckingham: Open University Press, 1992).

labour markets. In other words, the individual's class is determined by the opportunities presented to that individual in terms of earning opportunities and the level of possession of goods.

Looked at in this way, it would appear that the individual's consumption pattern is as much a determining factor of social class as it is the result of social class. Those individuals who are able to accumulate possessions and to improve their opportunities to earn money can move up the social scale. For example, a bricklayer would clearly be classified as working class (skilled manual worker). Yet if that same bricklayer saves some capital and sets up his own business, he could eventually become a wealthy property developer and thus be redefined as middle class (managerial or professional). This type of *social mobility* is becoming more commonplace as the old class barriers break down.

From the viewpoint of the marketer, social class is more a reflection of the existence of a set of *subcultures* based on the education level, occupational requirements and economic power of the individual members. In this context, marketers use class-related imagery in advertising in order to involve the consumer. For example, Mars bar advertisements show people in working-class occupations and leisure situations enjoying the Mars bar. Likewise, advertisements such as those for Nescafé Gold Blend use images of people in middle-class contexts to convey the impression that Gold Blend is the appropriate coffee for such people.

Within this cultural context, there is some evidence that the C2DE socioeconomic groups appear to be more conservative in their eating habits, and this was used with some success by Wall's when it introduced microwaveable ready meals. These meals were made to traditional British recipes, and were launched when it became clear that microwave ownership had reached a substantial proportion of the C2DE group.

Overall, social class still has some relevance to marketing activities, but increasing social mobility and a steady reduction in wealth concentration are eroding the old distinctions between classes, and reducing the cultural differences between them.

Key points from this chapter

This chapter has been about the environment within which decisions are made. This includes the physical and social environments, and the cultural and class contexts within which the consumer must function. The key points are as follows:

- Situation consists of physical surroundings, social surroundings, time, task and antecedent state.
- Advertising clutter results in avoidance of the advertisements by consumers.
- Warm colours work best for the outside of shops; cool colours for the insides.
- Disposition situations can be as important as use situations for marketers.
- Marketing communications are deeply culturally based, and therefore do not cross borders well.
- Social class is becoming harder to define due to social mobility, but still has some relevance in terms of defining a subculture.

Notes

1. Russell W. Belk, 'Situational variables and consumer behaviour', *Journal of Consumer Research*, vol. 2 (December 1975), pp. 159–64.
2. *Ibid.*
3. Michael L. Ray and Peter H. Webb, 'Three prescriptions for clutter', *Journal of Advertising Research*, vol. 26 (February–March 1986), pp. 69–78.
4. Joseph A. Bellizzi, Ayn E. Crowley and Ronald W. Hasty, 'The effects of colour in store design', *Journal of Retailing*, vol. 59 (Spring 1983), pp. 21–45.
5. R.E. Nisbett and D.E. Kanouse, 'Obesity, food deprivation and supermarket shopping behaviour', *Journal of Personality and Social Psychology*, vol. 12 (August 1969), pp. 289–94.
6. Peter R. Dickson, 'Person–situation: segmentation's missing link', *Journal of Marketing*, vol. 6 (Fall 1982). p. 57.

7. Gert Hofstede, *Culture's Consequences: International Differences in Work-Related Values* (Beverly Hills, CA: Sage, 1984).
8. Paul Herbig, William Koehler and Ken Day, 'Marketing to the baby bust generation', *Journal of Consumer Marketing*, vol. 10, no. 1 (1993), pp. 4–9.
9. Grant McCracken, 'Culture and consumption: a theoretical account of the structure and movement of the cultural meaning of consumer goods', *Journal of Consumer Research*, vol. 13 (June 1986), pp. 71–81.
10. John Clarke, 'Style', in Stuart Hall and Tony Jefferson (eds.), *Resistance through Rituals* (London: Hutchinson, 1976).
11. Dick Hebdige, *Subculture: The Meaning of Style* (London: Routledge, 1979).
12. Richard Scase, *Class* (Buckingham: Open University Press, 1992).
13. G. Marshall, H. Newby, R. Rose and C. Vogler, *Social Class in Modern Britain* (London: Hutchinson, 1988).
14. J. Goldthorpe, 'Women and class analysis: in defence of the conventional view', *Sociology*, vol. 17, no. 4 (1983), pp. 465–88.
15. Max Weber, 'Class, status, party', published posthumously in Hans H. Gerth and C. Wright Mills (eds.), *From Max Weber* (Oxford: Oxford University Press, 1946).

7

Peer and reference groups, and the family

This chapter is about the ways that people are influenced by the other people around them. This includes family, friends and the other groups with whom the individual has to interact.

After reading this chapter, you should be able to:

- Explain how reference groups affect purchasing behaviour.
- Describe how families make purchasing decisions.
- Explain the role of word-of-mouth communications in marketing.
- Develop tactical ways of making best use of word-of-mouth communication.

Peer and reference groups

A *group* is two or more persons who share a set of norms and whose relationship makes their behaviour interdependent. A *reference group* is 'A person or group of people that significantly influences an individual's behaviour'.[1] The reference groups provide standards or norms by which consumers judge their attitudes and behaviour.

Originally, groups formed for the purpose of co-operating on survival activities. Because human beings could co-operate in such activities as hunting, food gathering and defence from predators, we were able to increase the chances of survival for the species as a whole. Interestingly, this still appears to hold true: social researchers have reported that socially isolated people have mortality rates between 50 per cent and 300 per cent higher than people who are strongly integrated into groups.[2]

Most people prefer to fit in with the group (to a greater or lesser extent). This is either through politeness or through a desire not to be left out of things. Particularly with groups of friends, people will 'go along with the crowd' on a great many issues, and will tend to adopt the group norms regarding behaviour and attitudes. Experiments conducted by Solomon Asch in 1951 demonstrated this in a graphic manner.[3] In the experiment, subjects were asked to judge the lengths of different lines. The lines were displayed on a large board, and each person was seated with a group of strangers who were also supposed to be making judgements about the line lengths. In fact the strangers were Asch's assistants who had been instructed to agree with each other about the length of each line, but to make errors; the experimental subjects consistently agreed with these errors, even though the errors were sometimes glaringly obvious. Respondents did not make the same mistakes when there were no other people present, however. It appears from this that the fear of seeming foolish or of being the odd one out is enough to make the individual doubt the evidence of his or her eyes, or at the very least to lie about the evidence.

Reference groups fall into many possible groupings; the following list is not intended to be exhaustive.

Primary groups are composed of those people we see most often: friends, family, close colleagues. A primary group is small enough to permit face-to-face interaction on a regular basis, and there is cohesiveness and mutual participation, which result in similar beliefs and behaviour within the group. Because people tend to choose friends who think in similar ways, and have similar interests, the primary group is often very cohesive and long-lasting. Possibly the strongest primary group is the family, but the primary groups might be close friends, colleagues in work, or people with whom we share a hobby.

Secondary groups are composed of people we see occasionally, and with whom we have some shared interest. For example, a trade association or a sports club would constitute a secondary group. These groups are correspondingly less influential in shaping attitudes and controlling behaviour, but can exert influence on behaviour within the purview of the subject of mutual interest. For example, if you are a member of a cycling club, you may be persuaded to take part in a sponsored bike ride, or perhaps a protest in favour of creating more cycle lanes. Within a secondary group, primary groups will sometimes form; there will often be groups of special friends whose shared interests go beyond those of the rest of the secondary group. For example, a cycling enthusiast might say, 'This is my best mate, John. We went on a lads' weekend in Amsterdam last month with a bunch of mates from the pub. Yeah, John and I met through the cycling club.' In this example, the friends met through a secondary group (the cycling club) and formed a primary group to enjoy a different shared interest (the trip to Amsterdam).

Aspirational groups are the groups which the individual wants to join. These groups can be very powerful in influencing behaviour, because the individual will often adopt the behaviour of the aspirational group in the hopes of being accepted as a member. Sometimes the aspirational group will be better off financially, or will be more powerful; the desire to join such groups is usually classed as ambition. For example, a humble office worker may dream of one day having the key to the executive washroom. Advertising commonly uses images of aspirational groups, implying that use of a particular product will move the individual a little closer to being a member of an aspirational group.

Dissociative groups, on the other hand, are those groups which the individual does not want to be associated with. Like a backpacker who does not want to look like a typical tourist, or a lawyer who does not want to be taken for a Yuppie, the individual tries to avoid dissociative groups. This can have a negative effect on behaviour: the individual avoids certain products or behaviours rather than be taken for somebody from the dissociative group. Like aspirational groups, the definition of a group as dissociative is purely subjective; it varies from one individual to the next.

Formal groups have a known list of members, very often recorded somewhere. An example might be a professional association, or a club. Usually the rules and structure of the group are laid down in writing; there are rules for membership, and members' behaviour is constrained while they remain part of the group. However, the constraints usually apply only to fairly limited areas of behaviour: for example, the Chartered Institute of Marketing lays down a code of practice for marketers in their professional dealings, but has no interest in what its members do as private citizens. Membership of such groups may confer special privileges, such as job advancement or use of club facilities, or may only lead to responsibilities in the furtherance of the group's aims.

Informal groups are less structured, and are typically based on friendship. An example would be an individual's circle of friends, which only exists for mutual moral support, company and sharing experiences. Although there can be even greater pressure to conform than would be the case with a formal group, there is nothing in writing. Often informal groups expect a more rigorous standard of behaviour across a wider range of activities than would a formal group; such circles of friends are likely to develop rules of behaviour and traditions that are more binding than written rules.

Automatic groups are those groups to which one belongs by virtue of age, gender, culture or education. These are sometimes also called *category groups*. Although at first sight it would appear that these groups would not exert much influence on the members' behaviour, because they are groups which have not been joined voluntarily, it seems that people are influenced by group pressure to conform. For example, when buying clothes older people are sometimes reluctant to look like 'mutton dressed as lamb'.

Table 7.1 Influence of reference groups

Type of influence	Definition	Explanation	Example
Normative compliance	The pressure exerted on an individual to conform and comply	This works best when social acceptance is a strong motive, strong pressures exist from the group, and the product or service is conspicuous in its use.	Street gangs require their members to wear specific jackets, or other uniform. The members want to be accepted, the pressure to wear the jacket is great, and the jacket itself is a conspicuous badge of membership.
Value-expressive influence	The pressure that comes from the need for psychological association with a group	The desired outcome is respect from others; this pressure comes from the need for esteem, rather than from the need to belong.	The businessman in his pinstripe suit, the hippy in his colourful shirt, sweatband and jeans are both seeking respect from others by expressing a set of values in the way they dress.
Informational influence	The influence arising from a need to seek information from the reference group about the product category being considered	People often need to get expert advice and opinion about their product choices. This can often be provided by the appropriate reference group.	Many professional organizations and trade bodies offer their members free advice about useful products for their businesses. Clearly a recommendation on, say, computer software for a hairdressing business would be well received if it came from the Hairdressers Federation.

Source: After James F. Engel, Roger D. Blackwell and Paul W. Miniard, *Consumer Behaviour* (Fort Worth, TX: Dryden Press, 1995), chapter 20.

The above categories of group are not mutually exclusive. A dissociative group could also be an informal one; a formal group can be a secondary group (and often is) and so forth. For example, one may not wish to become friends with a group of drunken hooligans (who see themselves as an informal group of friends having a good time). Likewise the golf club could be a place of refuge to which one retreats to have a quiet drink with like-minded people, as well as a place where golf is played.

Reference groups affect consumer choice in three ways, as shown in Table 7.1. Of these influences, *normative compliance* is probably the most powerful. The source of normative compliance lies in *operant conditioning*: the individual finds that conforming behaviour results in group approval and esteem, whereas non-conforming behaviour results in group disapproval. Eventually the 'good' behaviour becomes automatic and natural, and it would be difficult to imagine any other way of doing things (see Chapter 4 for more on operant conditioning). The principles of good moral behaviour are not absolutes; they are the result (in most cases) of normative compliance with a reference group.

Of course, the pressure to conform will only work on someone who has a strong motivation to be accepted. If the pressure is coming from an aspirational group, this is likely to be the case; if, on the other hand, the pressure is coming from a dissociative group, the reverse will be the case and the individual will not feel under any pressure to conform. For example, most law-abiding citizens would comply with instructions from the police, and would usually go out of their way to help the police. Criminals, on the other hand, might avoid helping the police even in circumstances where their own crimes were not at issue.

The conspicuousness of the product or service is also crucial to the operation of normative compliance. For example, if all your friends vote Labour, you might be under some pressure to do likewise; but since the ballot is secret, nobody will know if you vote Conservative instead, so there is little pressure for normative compliance. Likewise, if all your friends drink Red Stripe lager, you may feel under pressure to do the same, but might be happy with supermarket own-brand when you are having a beer in the back garden at home.

Advertisers often appeal to the need to belong to an aspirational group. The TV campaign for Pepsi Max, in which a group of young men boast of their adventurous sporting accomplishments, is an example of this. The campaign is intended to appeal to those who see the group as exciting, and would like to belong.

Normative compliance is in decline in the western world due to the shifting social paradigm towards a more *inner-directed* society.[4] The reduction in face-to-face interaction may be leading to this move away from normative compliance; increasingly people communicate by impersonal means such as telephone, E-mail and fax. Whether this is a cause of the paradigm shift or one of its effects is difficult to decide at present.

The reference group will not exert influence over every buying decision. Even in circumstances where group influence does come into play, the consumer will be influenced by other variables, such as product characteristics, standards of judgement and conflicting influences from other groups. Table 7.2 shows some of the determinants of reference group influence.

Modelling was briefly discussed in Chapter 4, with regard to motivation and vicarious learning. The effectiveness of the role-model in modelling behaviour will depend on the personal characteristics of the role-model. *Attractive* models will be imitated more than unattractive ones, *successful-looking* models are given more credence than unsuccessful-looking ones, and a model who is perceived as being *similar* to the observer is also more likely to be emulated.[5]

Table 7.2 Determinants of reference group influence

Determinant	Definition	Explanation	Example
Judgement standards	The criteria used by the individual to evaluate the need to conform	Judgement standards are *objective* when the group norms are obvious and when the group approach is clearly the sensible course of action. The standards are *subjective* when it is not clear which is the most sensible course of action.	Decisions of the Cabinet are often portrayed as being unanimous; the Conservative Party is famous for presenting a united front, and individual members of the Cabinet therefore believe it is important to conform. The Labour Party, on the other hand, has a tradition of public debate and therefore its shadow Cabinet is more likely to disagree in public, since members do not see a need to conform.
Product characteristics	The features of the product that are salient to the group influence	The two main characteristics necessary for group influence to work are that the product should be *visible*, and that it should stand out (*non-universal ownership*)	During the 1980s the mobile phone became the symbol of the yuppie. First, it was obvious when in use because it was almost invariably used in public places, and second, it was something that not everybody had.
Member characteristics	The traits of the group member which make him or her more or less susceptible to group pressures	People vary considerably in the degree to which they are influenced by the pressures from the group. Some people remain fairly independent, where others conform habitually. Personality, status and security all seem to play major roles in determining whether an individual will conform or not.	It transpires that university students are much more likely to conform with group norms than housewives.[a] This is possibly because the university students are young, poor and away from home, so they have a greater need to belong.
Group characteristics	The features of the group that influence individuals to conform	The power of the group to influence the individual varies according to size, cohesiveness and leadership. Once the group is bigger than three members, the power to influence levels off. This is probably because the group has difficulty reaching a consensus. Likewise, the stronger the leadership the greater the influence, and the greater the cohesiveness the stronger the influence, because the group reaches a clear decision.	Most smokers take up the habit as a result of peer group pressure when they are aged around twelve or thirteen. If a child's friends are strongly anti-smoking, the influence from advertisers and even family background is likely to be much less of an influence.
Role-model	An individual whose influence is similar to that of a group	A role-model is a hero, a star or just somebody the individual respects and admires, and wishes to imitate.	When the *Starsky and Hutch* cop show first became popular on UK TV in the 1970s, it was noticeable that some traffic police began to wear their gloves with the cuffs rolled back, in imitation of the TV cops. Even earlier, when Clark Gable took off his shirt in a movie and showed that he was not wearing a vest, sales of vests plummeted because it became non-macho to wear one.

[a]Park, C.W. and Lessig, V.P., 'Students and housewives: susceptibility to reference group influence', *Journal of Consumer Research*, vol. 4 (September 1977), pp. 102–10.

There is also some evidence to show that observers are more likely to identify with role-models who have some difficulty in completing the modelled task.[6] In the Starsky and Hutch example given in Table 7.2, the TV cops always got their man in the end – but usually suffered considerable difficulties along the way. There has, of course, been considerable debate about whether crime shows on TV encourage people to copy the behaviour modelled; according to the theory, modelled behaviour will be copied if the observer feels able to identify with the role-model. Presumably, therefore, a programme showing young working-class men making a living from selling hard drugs might encourage other young working-class men to do the same. However, the saving grace of this scenario is that the role-model must also be seen to be successful and attractive – and in most shows the criminal is shown as being, ultimately, unsuccessful.

The family

Of all the reference groups, the family is probably the most powerful in influencing consumer decision making. The reasons for this are as follows:

- In the case of children, the parental influence is the earliest, and therefore colours the child's perception of everything that follows. In fact, the superego (see Chapter 3) is thought to be an internalized parent.
- In the case of parents, the desire to do the best they can for their children influences their decision making when making purchases for the family. Clear examples are the purchase of breakfast cereals such as Ready Brek, and disposable nappies, where the appeal is almost invariably to do with the comfort and well-being of the baby.
- In the case of siblings, the influence comes either as role-model (where the sibling is older) or as carer/adviser (where the sibling is younger).

Within the UK, a family is usually defined in narrow terms – the parents and their offspring. However, in most families there will also be influences from uncles, aunts, grandparents and cousins. While these influences are often less strong in UK households than they might be in some other countries where the extended family is more common, the influences still exist to a greater or lesser extent. One of the changes currently occurring throughout western Europe is the increase in the number of single-person households;[7] there is, of course, a difference between a household and a family. A further change, coming about through the tremendous increase in the divorce rate, is the growing number of single-parent families.

From a marketing viewpoint, the level of demand for many products is dictated more by the number of households than by the number of families. The relevance of families to marketing is therefore much more about consumer *behaviour* than about consumer *demand levels*.

In terms of its function as a reference group, the family is distinguished by the following characteristics:

- *Face-to-face contact.* Family members see each other every day or thereabouts, and interact as advisers, information providers and sometimes deciders. Other reference groups rarely have this level of contact.

- *Shared consumption.* Durables such as fridges, freezers, televisions and furniture are shared, and food is collectively purchased and cooked (although there is a strong trend away from families eating together). Purchase of these items is often collective; children even participate in decision making on such major purchases as cars and houses. Other reference groups may share some consumption (for example, a model railway club may hire a workshop and share tools) but families share consumption of most domestic items.

- *Subordination of individual needs.* Because consumption is shared, some family members will find that the solution chosen is not one that fully meets their needs (hence the Kia advertising campaign showing how the family car turns into a rally car – meeting the need of the father of the family to drive a sporty vehicle, while still meeting the family need for a school bus). Although this happens in other reference groups, the effect is more pronounced in families.

- *Purchasing agent.* Because of the shared consumption, most families will have one member who does most, or all, of the shopping. Traditionally, this has been the mother of the family, but increasingly the purchasing agents are the older children of the family – even pre-teens are sometimes taking over this role. The reason for this is the increase in the number of working mothers – women who work outside the home – which has left less time for shopping. This has major implications for marketers, since pre-teens and young teens generally watch more TV than adults and are therefore more open to marketing communications. Other reference groups may well have a purchasing agent, but this is probably only for specific items rather than for all those items the group is interested in – and most informal groups would only appoint a purchasing agent for occasional purposes (for example, to send out for pizza or to book a weekend away).

Family decision making is not as straightforward as marketers have supposed in the past. There has been an assumption that the purchasing agent (e.g. the mother) is the one who makes the decisions, and while this is often the case, this approach ignores the ways in which the purchase decisions are arrived at.

There is a problem here with terminology: traditionally, studies of the family have referred to the male partner as the husband, and the female partner as the wife. The increasing number of families in which the parents are not married has rendered this approach obsolete; however, the research reported in this section was conducted in the 1970s, when the vast majority of parents were married. The validity and relevance of the research is not in question, since it refers to traditional roles; these roles may or may not actually be adopted by specific families.

Role specialization is critical in family decision making because of the sheer number of different products that must be bought each year in order to keep the family supplied. What this means in practice is that, for example, the family member responsible for doing the cooking is also likely to take the main responsibility for shopping for food. The family member who does the most driving is likely to make the main decision about the car and its accessories, servicing, fuelling and so forth; the family gardener buys the gardening products, and so on.

Four kinds of marital role specialization have been identified: *wife dominant*, where the wife has most say in the decision; *husband dominant*, where the husband plays the major role; *syncratic* or *democratic*, where the decision is arrived at jointly; and *autonomic*, where the decision is made entirely independently of the partner.[8] For example, the wife may have the biggest role in deciding on new curtains, the husband may have the lead role in choosing the family car, they both may decide on a home extension, and the husband alone might choose the fertilizer for the garden. Marketers need to identify which role specialization type is mainly operating within a target market in order to know where to aim the promotional activities.

Product category affects role specialization and decision-making systems. When an expensive purchase is being considered, it is likely that most of the family will be involved in some way, if only because major purchases affect the family budgetting for other items. At the other end of the scale, day-to-day shopping for toilet rolls and cans of beans entails very little collective decision making. Where the product has a shared usage (a holiday or a car) the collective decision making component is likely to increase greatly. Conversely, where the product is used predominantly by one family member, that member will dominate the decision making even when the purchase is a major one (the family chef will make most of the decision about the new cooker, for example).

Culture has a marked effect on family decision-making styles. Religion and nationality will often affect the way decisions are made: African cultures tend to be male dominated in decision making, whereas European and North American cultures show a more egalitarian pattern of decision making.[9]

There are two issues here for the marketer: first, what is the effect on the marketing mix of the multiethnic society now emerging in the UK; and second, what is the effect when dealing internationally? This is a somewhat sensitive area, and one which marketers are still getting to grips with. There is more on the general aspects of culture in Chapter 6.

Social class creates patterns of decision making. Among very wealthy families, there appears to be a greater tendency for the husbands to make the decisions, but at the same time the norms of purchase tend to be well established and therefore discussion is unnecessary.[10] Lower-class families, with low incomes, tend to be more matriarchal, with the wives often handling the financial decisions about rent, insurance, food bills and Christmas clubs without reference to the husbands. Middle-class families tend to show greater democratic involvement in decision making. These social class distinctions are gradually breaking down, however, as a result of increasing wealth and mass education.

The family may well adopt different roles according to the *decision-making stage*. At the problem recognition stage of, for example, the need for new shoes for the children, the children themselves may be the main contributors. The mother may then decide what type of shoes should be bought, and the father may be the one who takes the children to buy the shoes. It is reasonable to suppose that the main user of the product might be important in the initial stages, with perhaps joint decision making at the final purchase.

Other determinants might include such factors as whether both parents are earning. Where they are, decision making is more likely to be joint because each has a financial stake in the outcome. Some studies seem to indicate that family decision making is more likely to be husband dominated when the husband is the sole earner, whereas couples who are both earning make decisions jointly.[11] Males also tend to dominate highly technical durable products (e.g. home computers).

Gender role orientation is clearly crucial to decision making. Husbands (and wives) with conservative views about gender roles will tend towards the assumption that most decisions about expenditure will be made by the husband. Even within this type of decision-making system, however, husbands will usually adjust their own views to take account of their wife's attitudes and needs.

Conflict resolution tends to have an increased importance in family decision making as opposed to individual purchase behaviour. The reason for this is that, obviously, more people are involved, each with their own needs and their own internal conflicts to resolve. The conflict resolution system is laid out in Table 7.3.

Table 7.3 Conflict resolution methods

Resolution method	Explanation
Persuasion through information exchange	When a conflict occurs, each family member seeks to persuade the others of his or her point of view. This leads to discussion, and ultimately some form of compromise.
Role expectation	If persuasion does not work, a family member may be designated to make the decision. This is usually somebody who has the greatest expertise in the area of conflict being discussed. This method appears to be going out of fashion as greater democracy in family decision making is appearing.
Establishment of norms	Families will often adopt rules for decision making. Sometimes this will involve taking turns over making decisions (perhaps over which restaurant the family will go to this week, or where they will go on holiday).
Power exertion	This is also known as browbeating. One family member will try to exert power to force the other members to comply; this may be a husband who refuses to sign the cheque unless he gets his own way, or a wife who refuses to cook the dinner until the family agree, or a child who throws a tantrum. The person with the most power is called the *least dependent person* because he or she is not as dependent on the other family members. Using the examples above, if the wife has her own income, she will not need to ask the husband to sign the cheque; if the other family members can cook, they can get their own dinner; and if the family can ignore the yelling toddler long enough, eventually the child will give up.

Source: Adapted from Sak Onkvisit and John J. Shaw, *Consumer Behaviour, Strategy and Analysis* (New York: Macmillan, 1994), chapter 12.

Influence of children on buying decisions

First-born children generate more economic impact than higher-order babies. Around 40 per cent of babies are first-born; they are photographed more, get all new clothes (no hand-me-downs) and receive more attention all round. First-born and only children have a higher achievement rate than their siblings, and since the birth rate is falling, there are more of them proportionally. More and more couples are choosing to have only one child, and families larger than two children are becoming a rarity. Childlessness is also more common now than it was 30 years ago.

Children also have a role in applying pressure to their parents to make particular purchasing decisions. The level of 'pester power' generated can be overwhelming, and parents will frequently give in to the child's demands.[12]

Although the number of children is steadily declining, their importance as consumers is not. Apart from the direct purchases of things that children need, they influence decision making to a marked extent. Children's development as consumers goes through five stages:

1. Observing.
2. Making requests.
3. Making selections.
4. Making assisted purchases.
5. Making independent purchases.

Recent research[13] has shown that pre-teens and young teens have a greater influence on family shopping choices than do the parents themselves, for these reasons:

- Often they do the shopping anyway, because both parents are working and the children have the available time to go to the shops.
- They watch more TV, so are more influenced by advertising and more knowledgeable about products.
- They tend to be more attuned to consumer issues, and have the time to shop around for (for example) free-range eggs.

The family is a flexible concept, and families go through life cycles. There have been various versions of the family life cycle, but most are based on the original work of Wells and Gubar.[14] Table 7.4 shows the stages of the family life cycle.

The family life cycle is a useful rule-of-thumb generalization, but given the high divorce rate and the somewhat uncertain nature of career paths, it is unlikely that many families would pass through all the stages quite as neatly as the model suggests. The model was developed in 1965 and 1966, and should therefore be treated with a degree of caution.

Gender roles

There are more women than men in the population, largely due to two factors: greater infant mortality among boys, and greater life expectancy of women.

Women's role has changed greatly over the past 30 years or so. Women now make more (or most) of the purchasing decisions, earn around a third of the household income, and make most of the decisions regarding the home and the children.

Major purchasing decisions are far more likely to be made jointly, and men are now much more likely to participate in decisions regarding the

Table 7.4 Family life cycle

Stage of life cycle	Explanation
Single stage	Single people tend to have low earnings, but also have low outgoings so have a high discretionary income. Tend to be more fashion and recreation orientated, spending on clothes, music, alcohol, eating out, holidays, leisure pursuits and hobbies, and 'mating game' products. Often buying cars and items for their first residence away from home.
Newly married couples	Newlyweds without children are usually dual-income households and therefore usually well-off. Still tend to spend on similar things to the singles, but also have the highest proportion of expenditure on household goods, consumer durables and appliances. Appear to be more susceptible to advertising.
Full nest I	When the first child arrives, one parent usually stops working outside the home, so family income drops sharply. The baby creates new needs which alter expenditure patterns: furniture and furnishings for the baby, baby food, vitamins, toys, nappies and baby food. Family savings decline, and couples are usually dissatisfied with their financial position.
Full nest II	The youngest child is over 6, so often both parents will work outside the home. The employed spouse's income has risen due to career progression, and the family's total income recovers. Consumption patterns still heavily influenced by children: bicycles, piano lessons, large-size packages of breakfast cereals, cleaning products, etc.
Full nest III	Family income improves as the children get older. Both parents are likely to be working outside the home, and both may have had some career progression; also, the children will be earning some of their own money from paper rounds, part-time jobs, etc. Family purchases might be a second car, replacement furniture, some luxury items and children's education.
Empty nest I	Children have grown up and left home. Couple are at the height of their careers and spending power, have low mortgages, very reduced living costs. Often go for luxury travel, restaurants and theatre, so they need fashionable clothing, jewellery, diets, spas, health clubs, cosmetics, hairdressing.
Empty nest II	Main breadwinner has retired, so some drop in income. Expenditure is more health orientated, buying appliances for sleep, over-the-counter remedies for indigestion. Often buy a smaller house or move to an apartment in Spain.
Solitary survivor	If still in the workforce, widows and widowers enjoy a good income. May spend more money on holidays, as well as the items mentioned in empty nest II.
Retired solitary survivor	Same general consumption pattern as above, but on a smaller scale due to reduced income. Has special needs for love, affection and security, so may join clubs, etc.

household expenditure. A recent American survey found that 35 per cent of couples said that they were equally responsible for food shopping; 8 per cent said the man was solely responsible; the other 57 per cent said the woman did the food shopping.[15] This is a marked change from the situation

30 years ago, when a man shopping for food would be a rarity (or a bachelor).

The change in gender roles comes from the following:

- Technology means that most jobs do not require physical strength, so more careers are open to women.
- Mass contraception has freed women from childbearing.
- A more ordered society has led to greater physical security; there is less need for the defence role of the male.
- More widespread education means that women are not satisfied to stay at home and do housework.

This shift in gender roles and expectations is affecting marketers, who are now changing the appeal of their advertising to meet the new conditions. For example, Nissan has been running a series of ads in which a woman punishes her man for borrowing her car, the hook line being 'Ask before you borrow it.' Robbie Coltrane is shown doing the washing up with Persil washing-up liquid, Barclay's Mastercard is shown as being the way that real men buy the food for a dinner party, and the new MD of Kenco Coffee is portrayed as a woman who skilfully handles sexist comments from men all over the world. Even twenty years ago such advertisements would only have been shown for comic purposes, and even now men are frequently portrayed as being incapable of doing the housework properly (e.g. in the Mastercard ad the punchline is that the woman has sent out for pizza 'as a back-up' in case the man fails to buy the food).

Eventually one might expect that gender role will not be an issue in advertising at all, but since advertising (at least in part) reflects society, this may still be some way off.

Mechanisms of personal influence

Groups and individuals obviously have a strong influence on people's attitudes and behaviour. There are three main theories regarding the mechanisms whereby this personal influence is exerted. The history of the theory is not so much one of advancing knowledge about the mechanisms involved, but rather a history of the way society has changed in the period in which the theories were evolving.

Trickle-down theory (see Figure 7.1) says that lower-class people often imitate upper-class people.[16] Influence is transmitted down from the wealthier classes to the poorer classes, as the poorer groups in society seek to 'better themselves'. In fact, trickle-down is rarely seen in industrialized,

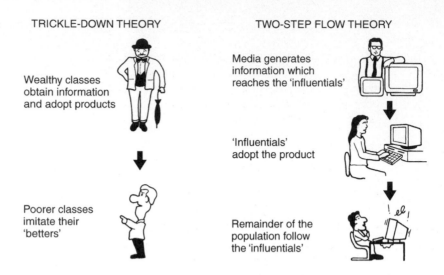

Figure 7.1 Trickle-down vs two-step flow theory

wealthy countries like the UK because new ideas are disseminated over-night by the mass media and copied by chain stores within days. This is particularly true of clothing fashions, and the Punk revolution in the mid-1970s was an example of 'trickle-up', where the fashion came up from the poorer classes. What is replacing trickle-down theory is *homophilous influence*, which refers to transmission between those of similar age, education, social class, etc.: in other words, those who already have a lot in common.

Two-step flow theory (also in Figure 7.1) says that new ideas flow from the media to 'influentials', who then pass the information on to the rest of society.[17] When this theory was first formulated in the late 1940s and early 1950s, it probably had a great deal of truth in it, and there is still evidence for this view; certainly in the diffusion of innovative high-tech products there is strong evidence for it. However, there is a weakening of this mechanism due to the preponderance of mass media. In the 1940s, most homes did not have TV and there was no commercial radio in the UK; the availability of commercial information was therefore more restricted to the wealthy. Also, the two-step flow assumes that the audience is passively waiting for the information to be presented, whereas in fact people actively seek out information about new things by asking friends and relatives and by looking for published information.

The *multistage interaction* model (Figure 7.2) agrees that some people are more influential than others, but also recognizes that the mass media affect both influential and seeker. The influential does not mediate the informa-tion flow, as the two-step model suggests, but rather acts as a mechanism

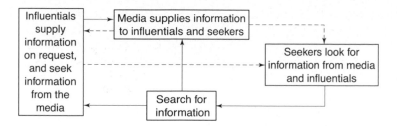

Figure 7.2 Multistage interaction model

Table 7.5 Characteristics of influentials

Characteristic	Description of influential
Demographics	Wide differences according to product category. For fashions and film going young women dominate. For self-medication, women with children are most influential. Generally, demography shows low correlation and is not a good predictor.
Social activity	Influencers and opinion leaders are usually gregarious.
General attitudes	Generally innovative and positive towards new products.
Personality and lifestyle	Low correlation of personality with opinion leadership. Lifestyle tends to be more fashion conscious, more socially active, more independent.
Product related	Influencers are more interested in the specific product area than are others. They are active searchers and information gatherers, especially from the mass media.

Source: Adapted from James F. Engel, Roger D. Blackwell and Paul W. Miniard, *Consumer Behaviour* (Fort Worth, TX: Dryden Press, 1995).

for emphasizing or facilitating the information flow. Within the model, there is a continuous dialogue between marketers, seekers and influentials, with many stages of influence before the new idea is adopted or rejected.

Clearly it is important for marketers to identify who the influential people are likely to be, and much research has been carried out into this area. Table 7.5 shows the main characteristics of influentials which have been identified so far. However, this is probably not an exhaustive list; nor will it be generally applicable to all cases.

Influencers (and others) like to pass on their knowledge, and there are several reasons for doing this.

- *Involvement* is a major force. The influencer is actually interested in the subject area, and wants to share the excitement with others. A hi-fi enthusiast who buys a new Arcam stereo will want to tell friends and colleagues all about it on Monday morning. Telling other people acts as an outlet for the pleasure of owning the equipment.

- *Self-enhancement* is about airing one's superior knowledge. People like to appear to be 'in the know' – perhaps being able to say, 'I discovered a wonderful unspoiled place for a holiday.' Appearing to be a connoisseur, whether of fine wines or works of art or classic cars, is something many influencers strive for.

- *Concern for others* often precipitates influence. The genuine desire to help a friend to reach a good decision often prompts the expert to say, 'OK, I'll come with you when you go to the shop.' This factor works most strongly when there is a strong link between the people involved, and when the influencer has been very satisfied with the product or service concerned.

- *Message intrigue* is the factor concerned with comments about advertising messages. If an advertisement is particularly intriguing or humorous, people will discuss it; this enhances the message by repetition. A prime example of this is the long series of advertisements for Hamlet cigars which was only ended on UK TV by a Europe-wide ban on tobacco advertising. In each case the hero's disappointment when life turned out badly was assuaged by smoking a Hamlet to the accompaniment of Jacques Loussier's piano. These advertisements were widely quoted and even now pianists can raise a smile by playing the opening bars of the Loussier arrangement.

- *Dissonance reduction* is about reducing doubts after making a major purchase. As word-of-mouth influence, this can be good or bad: sometimes the influencer will try to reassure him or herself by telling everybody about the good points of the product; more often, though, the disappointed customer will use word-of-mouth to complain bitterly and explain how the wicked manufacturer has cheated him or her. This is sometimes a way of passing the responsibility over to the supplier rather than admitting that the influencer has made a bad decision or a bad choice.

Overall, word-of-mouth influence is much stronger than advertising or other marketer-produced communications. For marketers, then, the problem lies in knowing how to use word-of-mouth to its best advantage. Table 7.6 offers some comparisons and strategies.

It is not usually possible to rely entirely on word-of-mouth, but marketers should take steps to stimulate it as a promotional tool. If you are in a position to be able to identify influentials, it is well worthwhile offering to lend them the product (or even give them it, if the cost is low enough), so that they can be stimulated into talking about it to friends. Advertising should be interesting and involving, perhaps even controversial (as Benetton has tried to be), so that debate ensues. Although it is not true to say that any word-of-mouth will be good for a company, it is certainly true

Table 7.6 Power of word-of-mouth influences

Strong influence	Weak influence	Tactical suggestions
Seeker initiates conversation with source	Source initiates conversation with seeker	Advertising could emphasize the idea of 'Ask the person who owns one'. Network marketers could emphasize a more advisory role for their salespeople rather than a strongly proactive approach.
Negative information	Positive information	Because marketers are uniformly positive about the product, the seeker is more alert to any negatives. The essential thing for marketers to do is to ensure that any complaints are dealt with immediately and thoroughly (see Chapter 3).
Verbal communication is stronger for thinking and evaluation	Visual communication is stronger for awareness and stimulation of interest	Where appropriate, marketers could encourage satisfied customers to show their friends the product; this tactic is often used for home improvement sales, where customers are paid a small reward or commission for introducing friends to the product. This is also the basis for party-plan selling, e.g. Tupperware and Anne Summers.

to say that controversy and debate will always increase brand awareness, even when it does not enhance brand image.

Car manufacturers usually give exceptionally generous discounts to car hire companies, taking the view that the hirer might well be tempted to buy the same model at a later stage.

To prevent negative word-of-mouth, marketers should do more than merely satisfy any customer complaints. Coca-Cola carried out a survey of customer communications in 1981.[18] The survey was undertaken among customers who had complained to the company. Here are the main findings:

- More than 12 per cent told twenty or more people about the company's response to their complaint.
- Those who were completely satisfied with the response told a median of four to five others about the experience.
- Nearly 10 per cent of those who reported being completely satisfied increased their purchases of company products.
- Those who thought their complaint was not dealt with fairly told a median of nine to ten other people.
- Of those who thought their complaint was not dealt with fairly, nearly one-third subsequently boycotted company products entirely, and another 45 per cent reduced their purchases.

From these figures it follows that marketers should actually encourage people to complain, and should go beyond the call of duty in satisfying complaints, since this will actually increase the loyalty of those who complain.

Key points from this chapter

In this chapter we have looked at some of the interpersonal factors which influence purchasing behaviour. In particular, we have looked at the groups and individuals who most influence consumers, and at the ways the influence is exerted. Finally, we have looked at ways that marketers can use these interpersonal factors to improve customer relations and customer loyalty. The key points from the chapter are as follows:

- Most people are members of several reference groups, all of which influence the individual in different ways.
- Normative compliance is probably the most powerful influence on behaviour.
- Conspicuousness is the most crucial product characteristic for normative compliance.
- Families share consumption, have face-to-face product information exchanges, subordinate personal need and delegate purchasing roles.
- Word-of-mouth spreads because the informant (influencer) likes to talk about the products concerned.
- Complaints can be turned to the marketer's advantage by generous handling.
- There is still a great deal of gender stereotyping in advertising, but much of it is showing male stereotypes in traditionally female roles.

Notes

1. William O. Beardon and Michael J. Etzel, 'Reference group influence on product and brand purchase decisions', *Journal of Consumer Research*, vol. 9 (September 1982), p. 184.
2. Gene Koretz, 'Economic trends', *Business Week*, 5 March 1990.
3. Solomon E. Asch, 'Effects of group pressure on the modification and distortion of judgements', in H. Guetzkow (ed.), *Groups, Leadership and Men* (Pittsburgh, PA: Carnegie Press, 1951).
4. W. Kirk McNulty, 'UK social change through a wide-angle lens', *Futures*, August 1985.

5. Michael J. Baker and Gilbert A Churchill, Jr, 'The impact of physically attractive models on advertising evaluations', *Journal of Marketing Research*, vol. 14 (November 1977), pp. 538–55.
6. Charles C. Manz and Henry P. Sims, 'Vicarious learning: the influence of modelling on organisational behaviour', *Academy of Management Review*, (January 1981), pp. 105–13.
7. European Commission, *General Statistics of the European Community 1991*.
8. Harry L. Davies and Benny P. Rigaux, 'Perception of marital roles in decision processes', *Journal of Consumer Research*, vol. 1 (June 1974), pp. 5–14.
9. Robert T. Green *et al.*, 'Societal development and family purchasing roles: a cross-national study', *Journal of Consumer Research*, vol. 9 (March 1983).
10. Mirra Komarovsky, 'Class differences in family decision-making', in Nelson N. Foote (ed.), *Household Decision Making* (New York: New York University Press, 1961).
11. Pierre Filiatrault and J.R. Brent Ritchie, 'Joint purchasing decisions: a comparison of influence structure in family and couple decision-making units', *Journal of Consumer Research*, vol. 7 (September 1980), pp. 131–40.
12. Karin M. Ekstrom, Patriya S. Tansuhaj and Ellen Foxman, 'Children's influence in family decisions and consumer socialisation: a reciprocal view', in Melanie Wallendorf and Paul Anderson (eds.), *Advances in Consumer Research*, vol. 14 (Provo, UT: Association for Consumer Research, 1987).
13. Anon., 'Teenage daughters of working mothers have a big role in purchase, brand-selection decisions', *Marketing News*, vol. 18 (February 1983), p. 20.
14. William D. Wells and George Gubar, 'The life cycle concept in marketing research', *Journal of Marketing Research*, vol. 3 (November 1966), pp. 353–63.
15. Opinion Research Corporation, 'Tarzan of the Foodmart', *American demographics*, vol. 12 (May 1990), p. 13.
16. Thorstein Veblen, *The Theory of the Leisure Class* (New York: Macmillan, 1899).
17. Paul F. Lazarsfield, Bernard R. Berelson and Hazel Gaudet, *The People's Choice* (New York: Columbia University Press, 1948).
18. *Measuring the Grapevine: Consumer response and word-of-mouth* (The Coca-Cola Company, 1981).

8

New and repeat buying behaviour

This chapter is concerned with the ways consumers approach making purchase decisions. The methods used depend on whether the purchase is a new one, or a repeat of a previous purchase; whether the product is novel or tried and tested; whether the purchase is routine or out of the ordinary.

After reading this chapter, you should be able to:

- Describe some of the main models of consumer decision-making processes.
- Explain the diffusion of innovation.
- Describe the differences between different types of innovation.
- Develop strategies for launching new products.

Decision-making models

Decision-making models are often complex and involve many stages. The John Dewey model[1] outlined in the early part of this century gives the following five stages:

1. A difficulty is felt (need identification).
2. The difficulty is located and defined.
3. Possible solutions are suggested.
4. Consequences are considered.
5. A solution is accepted.

This can be restated as follows:

1. Need recognition.
2. Pre-purchase activities or search.
3. Evaluation and purchase decision.
4. Act of purchase and consumption.
5. Post-purchase evaluation.

As explained in Chapter 1, need becomes apparent when there is a divergence of the desired and actual states. The motivation that arises from this depends on the level of disparity between the *actual state* and the *desired state*. For example, a driver who is late for an appointment may be thirsty, but not thirsty enough to stop the car at a motorway service station. Likewise, a householder might have run out of one or two items, but still has enough food in the house to get by on; as the days go by, more and more items are used up, and eventually a trip to the supermarket becomes essential. The disparity between the actual and desired states grows greater, in other words, and therefore the householder becomes more strongly motivated to do something about it.

There are two possible reasons for a divergence between the desired and the actual states: one is that the actual state changes; the other is that the desired state changes. In practice, it is rare for the actual states and the desired states to be the same, since this would imply that the consumer would be perfectly happy and have everything that he or she could possibly want, which is rarely the case in an imperfect world.

Causes of shift of the *actual* state might be from the following list:[2]

- *Assortment depletion*. Consumption, spoilage or wear and tear on the stock of goods or products within the individual's assortment.
- *Income change*. This can be upwards, through a salary increase or windfall, or downwards, through (say) redundancy.

Causes of shifts in the *desired* state often have more to do with marketing activities. This is because *new information* may change the individual's aspirations. If the individual sees a better car, hears a better stereo, or otherwise becomes aware that there is a better solution to the problem than the one currently in use, there is likely to be a shift in the desired state. From a marketing viewpoint, this approach is most effective when the consumers are not satisfied with their present products.

Changing desire is often brought on by a change in actual state: getting a new job may mean moving house, for example. Sometimes a pay increase (which is a shift in the actual state) will raise the individual's aspirations and he or she will consider purchases that previously had been out of reach and therefore not even considered. For example, a lottery win might prompt an individual to book the holiday of a lifetime somewhere.

The *psychology of complication* says that people complicate their lives deliberately by seeking new products, even though they are fairly satisfied with the old one. (This may account in part for the high divorce rate.) The psychology of complication is the opposite of the *psychology of simplification*, which says that consumers try to simplify their lives by making repeat purchases of the same old brand.[3] Probably both these mechanisms act on consumers at different times.

Conditions causing shifts in actual and desired states are interdependent: that is to say, a shift in the actual state (sudden redundancy, for example) will cause a shift in the desired state (instead of looking for a promotion, the individual would now be glad just to have a job at the old grade). Likewise a shift in the desired state (seeing a programme about a holiday in Sri Lanka and wanting to go there) will cause a shift in the actual state as soon as the consumer tries to save for the trip.

Pre-purchase activities

Having recognized the need, the consumer will undertake a series of pre-purchase activities.

The *information search* comes from two sources: an *internal* search (from memory), and an *external* search (from outside sources). In both cases most of the information originates from seller-based sources, and is therefore readily available and low cost. If the internal information search is insufficient – that is, the individual does not have enough knowledge of the product category to be able to make a choice – an external search will be undertaken.

Sometimes an individual will set out with the belief that he or she has sufficient internal information to make the purchase, but is then presented with new information at the point of purchase. For example, somebody who owned a cordless telephone ten years ago and would now like to buy another might already feel familiar with the product. On entering the shop, the individual might be presented with a staggering array of cordless telephones with features which were not available ten years ago, and which might even be incomprehensible. In that case the consumer may feel the need to ask questions of the shop assistants in order to gain enough information to make an informed decision. Incidentally, it is very common for people with limited information to base the decision on price simply because they lack the necessary understanding to make a judgement based on other features of the product.

Search efforts are not very extensive under most circumstances, even for major purchases like houses, because of the amount of time and effort that has to be expended. Usually consumers will continue to search until they

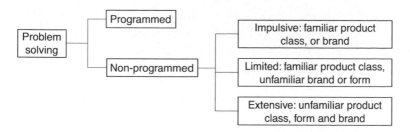

Figure 8.1 Classification of problem solving (Source: Sak Onkvisit and John J. Shaw, *Consumer Behaviour, Strategy and Analysis*, New York: Macmillan, 1994)

find something that is adequate to meet the need, and will then not look any further. For example, a US study[4] found that almost three-quarters of purchasers of insurance policies bought from the first company they saw.

Assortment adjustment is the act of entering the market to replenish or exchange the assortment of products that the consumer owns. Assortment adjustment can be *programmed* (habitual) or *non-programmed* (new purchases) (see Figure 8.1). Non-programmed assortment adjustment divides into three categories. *Impulse* purchases are not based on a plan, and usually just happen as the result of a sudden confrontation with a stimulus. Such purchases are not always of familiar products; sometimes consumers will spend quite substantial amounts on a whim, perhaps a sudden urge to buy a particularly attractive jacket or to buy a fancy electronic gadget. Impulse buying has been further subdivided into four categories:[5] *pure* impulse, based on the novelty of a product; *reminder* impulse, which relates to a product which has been left off the shopping list; *suggestion* impulse, which is about products that fulfil a previously unfelt need; and *planned* impulse, which occurs when the customer has gone out to buy a specific type of product, but is prepared to be swayed by special offers.

For example, a consumer may set out to the supermarket to buy the week's groceries, plus something for lunch today. On the way round, he sees a jar of almond-stuffed olives and decides to buy some to try (pure impulse). Next he notices the green lasagna, which reminds him that he is out of pasta (reminder impulse), and also on the shelf near it a special rack for keeping lasagna separate while it is cooking (suggestion impulse). Finally, he notices that the smoked chicken is on special offer, and decides to buy some for lunch (planned impulse). This type of scenario is familiar to most people who shop in supermarkets, and indeed supermarkets will often capitalize on this in the way the shelves are stocked and in the way the store is laid out.

The other two types of non-programmed decision making involve either limited decision making or extended decision making. Of the two, limited decision making is probably the most common.

Limited decision making takes place when the customer is already familiar with the product class and merely wants to update his or her information, or fill in a few gaps revealed by the internal search. This is typical behaviour for someone who is replacing a car: since this is usually an infrequent activity, consumers often find it necessary to check out what new models are available and renew acquaintance with the price levels being charged, even though (as a driver) the consumer will have considerable knowledge of what a car is and what it can be expected to do.

Limited decision making tends to occur when the consumer is not completely satisfied with the existing product and seeks a better alternative. Here the consumer is only looking for something that overcomes the perceived problem with the existing product.

Extended decision making occurs when the consumer is unfamiliar with the product class, form and brand. For example, for most people a mobile telephone would be a completely new class of product and they would have to undertake a fairly extensive information search before committing to a telephone or network. Extended decision making is caused by unfamiliarity: consumers who do not know much about the product category, brands, etc. will tend to shop around more.

Factors affecting the external search for information

The extent and nature of the external search for information will depend on a range of factors connected with the consumer's situation, the value and availability of the information, the nature of the decision being contemplated, and the nature of the individual. Figure 8.2 illustrates how these factors interrelate.

Assortment adjustment can take the form of either assortment *replenishment*, replacing worn-out or consumed products, or assortment *extension*, adding to the range of products owned. Assortment replenishment will usually require very little information searching or risk, since the product is already known. Assortment extension is more likely to lead to an extensive problem-solving pattern.

The type of problem solving adopted will depend on the task at hand. A *programmed* decision pattern will lead almost immediately to purchase; these are the regular, always-buy-the-same-brand type of decisions. *Nonprogrammed* decisions may still lead immediately to a purchase by impulse, but this type of decision pattern will more probably lead to limited or extensive information search patterns.

The *perceived value* of the information is important in terms of how extensive the information search will be. In other words, the extent of the

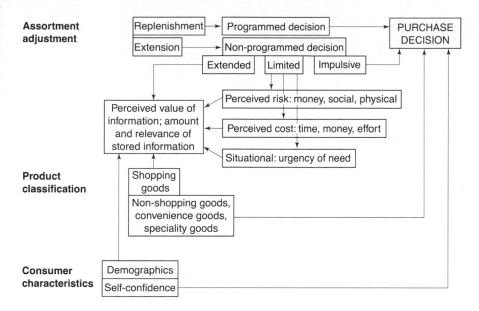

Figure 8.2 Factors affecting external search

external search depends on how valuable the information is. If there is plenty of information in the 'internal files' within the consumer's mind, the extent of external information seeking will be correspondingly less: consumers who are highly familiar with the product will search less than those who are only moderately familiar.[6]

The *relevance* of this information is also a factor: if it is a long time since the last purchase, the stored information may no longer be relevant. New alternatives may have developed or the product may have improved. If the consumer was satisfied with the last product (which may by now have been consumed or have worn out), the internal information will probably be regarded as relevant, and the search will be less extensive or non-existent.[7]

Any action by a consumer produces unpredictable consequences, some of which might be unpleasant.[8] These consequences form the *perceived risk* of the transaction. *Financial risk* is present since the consumer could lose money; for houses, cars and other major purchases the risk is great because the commitment is long term. Because the risk is reduced as knowledge increases, greater perceived risk will tend to lead to greater information search efforts, and the benefits of such a search will be correspondingly greater. If the consumer feels certain about the decision already, there will be correspondingly less benefit in carrying out a search for information.

The fear of losing face with friends and associates is the major component of *social risk*. It is determined in part by product visibility: consumers who buy certain eastern European cars can risk ridicule from their friends and colleagues, and might therefore carry out a more extended information search to ensure that the car will not provoke this reaction.

Perceived cost is the extent to which the consumer has to commit resources to the search. People will frequently cut the search down simply because it is taking too much time, money or effort. This is because the potential loss of making a wrong purchase decision is seen as being less than the cost of making a full search.

Time is a cost relating to search. It is sometimes measured in *opportunity cost*, or in terms of what the person could be doing instead of spending time searching. For example, highly paid people may value their time highly because they can earn more money at a desk than they save by shopping around, so they are prepared to spend money in order to save time. Poorer consumers may be more prepared to spend time shopping around in order to save money.[9]

Money costs are the out-of-pocket expenses of searching. Clearly a consumer who wants to buy olive oil might compare different brands in Tesco's, but is unlikely to drive to Sainsbury's to check their prices, and would certainly not cross the Channel to check the prices in Mammouth at Dieppe (even though olive oil would certainly be cheaper in Mammouth).

The *psychological costs* of the information search include frustration, driving, chasing around to different shops, talking to shop assistants, and generally giving a lot of thinking time to the search. Often the consumer will become overwhelmed with the quantity of information available, and will be unable to reach a decision because of information overload.

Sometimes the reverse happens and the consumer actually enjoys the shopping experience as an entertainment. *Ongoing search* is different from external search, in that consumers go to look for product information to augment stored product knowledge, and just for the fun of it. In other words, some people go shopping just for fun, and this is often a more important motivator than a genuine need to buy something.[10]

Situational factors will also affect the product information search. The search will be limited, for example, if there is an urgency for the product. If the car has broken down, the driver is unlikely to phone around for the cheapest breakdown van. Other variables might include product scarcity and lack of available credit.

In terms of *product classification*, *shopping goods* are those for which a new solution has to be formulated every time. *Non-shopping goods* are those for which the consumer already has a complete preference and specification, and the consumer almost always buys the same brand.[11] For example, tomato ketchup is usually a non-shopping product, whereas a stereo system is a shopping product.

Consumer characteristics are those features of the consumer which affect the information search. Demographics affect the search, in that *outshoppers* (people who shop outside the area in which they live) have higher incomes, and are mobile. This factor may be product specific, since outshopping most frequently occurs when buying groceries at an out-of-town shopping centre or buying consumer durables. Outshopping can also occur in the form of the shopping trip to London, or the 'booze cruise' to Calais.

Making the choice

Having gone through the procedures of collecting information, whether by a lengthy search or by simply remembering all the necessary facts, the consumer will make a choice based on the collected information. The first procedure is to establish a *consideration set*, which is the group of products from which the final choice is to be made. This consideration set will only usually contain a small subset of all the possible alternatives, so from the marketer's viewpoint it is essential to be included in the consideration set, and this is the role of much of the advertising activity undertaken.

Consumers construct the consideration set from the knowledge obtained in the information search. Consumers will often use *cut-offs*, or restrictions on the minimum or maximum acceptable values. Typically, consumers will have a clear idea of the price range they are willing to pay, for example, and any product priced outside this zone will not be included. Incidentally, this price range may have a minimum as well as a maximum: many executive-type car buyers will not want to be seen driving an old banger or a very cheap car. Again, marketers need to know what the consumer's cut-off point is on given specifications; this can be determined by market research.

Signals are important to consumers when judging product quality. A signal could be a brand name, a guarantee or even a price tag. It is very common for consumers to equate quality with a high price, so a useful tactic for low-priced manufacturers is to undermine this perception in as many ways as possible. The use of price as a quality signal is somewhat reduced when other signals are present. For example, if the consumer is easily able to judge the quality by inspecting the product, the relationship may not apply.

Finally, consumers will often select a *decision rule* or *heuristic*. Consumers develop these rules over a period of time: for example, a rule might be always to buy the best quality one is able to afford at the time. Some consumers have rules about brand names, or shops they know and trust, or people whose preferences they will always respect.

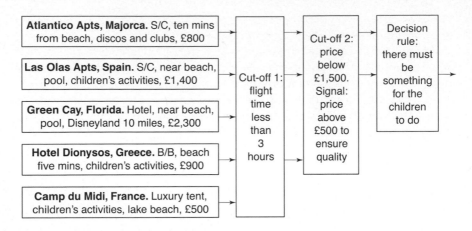

Figure 8.3 Decision-making process for a holiday purchase

Figure 8.3 shows an example of a decision-making process for a holiday purchase. According to the diagram, the consumer begins with a choice of five different holidays, which form the consideration set. The relevant information about each holiday has been included, and now the decision rules need to be applied. First of all, the consumer decides that a long flight would be difficult with children, so he or she sets a limit of three hours. This cuts out Greece and Florida. Then there is a cut-off on cost (not to go above £1,500). This cut-off has no relevance, since none of the remaining holidays costs above £1,500, but the consumer also uses price as a signal by which to judge quality, and cuts out the tent in France because it is too cheap. The remaining decision rule is that there must be something for the children to do, and this leaves only the apartment in Spain as the final choice.

Sometimes the consumer will find that applying all the decision rules cuts out all of the alternatives, so that a revision of the rules needs to take place. This can result in establishing a hierarchy of rules according to their relative importance.[12]

Categorization of decision rules

Non-compensatory decision rules are absolute: if a product does not meet the decision rule for one attribute, this cannot be compensated for by its strength in other areas. In the holiday example above, although the Florida location is near to Disneyland, and is therefore a very strong candidate as far as entertaining the children is concerned, the cost and the flight time rule it out. In the *lexicographic* approach, the consumer establishes a hierarchy of attributes, comparing products first against the most important attribute, then against the second most important, and so forth. In the holiday example, the consumer might feel that children's activities are the most important attribute, in which case the Florida destination might be the most attractive. Decisions can be made by *elimination of aspects*, whereby the product is examined against other brands according to attributes, but then each attribute is checked against a cut-off. In the above example, this led to Florida being rejected on grounds of flight time and cost.

The *conjunctive* rule is the last of the non-compensatory rules. Here each brand is compared in turn against all the cut-offs; only those brands which survive this winnowing-out will be compared with each other.

Compensatory decision rules allow for trade-offs, so that a weakness in one area can be compensated for in another. The *simple additive* rule involves a straight tally of the product's positive aspects, and a comparison of this tally with the tally for other products. The product with the most positive attributes will be the one chosen. A variation of this is the *weighted additive* approach, which gives greater weight to some attributes than to others. In each case, though, the products do not necessarily have to have all the attributes in common (or, indeed, any of them).

Phased decision strategies may involve using rules in a sequence. For example, the consumer may use a non-compensatory cut-off to eliminate products from the consideration set, then use a weighted additive rule to decide between the remaining products.

Two more special categories of decision rule exist. First, the consumer may need to create a *constructive decision rule*. This means establishing a rule from scratch when faced with a new situation. If the rule thus created works effectively, the consumer will store it in memory until the next time the situation is encountered, and 'recycle' the rule then. Second, *affect referral* is the process whereby consumers retrieve a 'standard' attitude from memory. For example, a consumer may not like Japanese cars, and this attitude prevents the inclusion of any Japanese car in the consideration set.

For marketers, it is clearly useful to know how consumers are approaching their decision making. If, for example, consumers are using a weighted additive rule, it would be useful to know which attributes are given the greatest weightings. If, however, consumers are using a conjunctive rule with cut-offs at known levels, the product can be designed to fall within the cut-offs. The initial aim for marketers must be to ensure that the product becomes part of the consideration set for most consumers, and therefore it must pass at least the first hurdles in terms of the cut-offs and signals employed in the decision process.

Several attempts have been made to bring the factors in consumer decision making together in one model. Most of these models are complex,

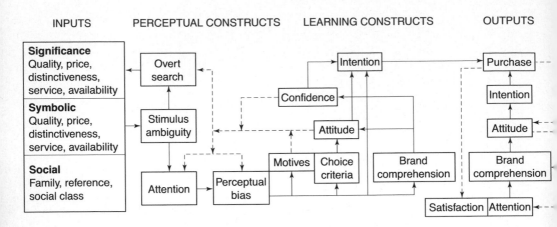

Figure 8.4 Howard–Sheth model of consumer behaviour (Source: Adapted from John A. Howard and Jagdish N. Sheth, *The Theory of Buyer Behaviour*, New York: John Wiley, 1969)

since there are many factors which interrelate in a number of ways; an example is the Howard–Sheth model shown in Figure 8.4. This is a somewhat simplified version; the original requires one diagram to be superimposed on another.

In the diagram, the solid arrows show the flow of information, while the dotted arrows show the feedback effects. Essentially, the diagram deals with the way the inputs are dealt with by perception and by learning, and eventually become outputs.

New products: the diffusion of innovation

Decision making and information gathering are at their most complex when consumers are considering an innovative product. Thousands of new products are launched on to the market every year, with varying success rates; the vast majority never recoup their development costs. (Estimates of new product success rates vary, largely due to the difficulty of defining what constitutes success.)

Products are constantly being superseded by newer, more effective products. For this reason, firms seek to develop new products; those firms that fail to innovate will, eventually, only be producing products that are obsolescent. The product life cycle in Figure 8.5 illustrates the process of introduction, growth, maturity and obsolescence in products.

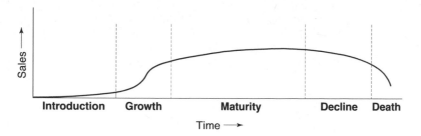

Figure 8.5 The product life cycle

The product life cycle can be explained in terms of consumer behaviour. In the introduction and growth stages, the more innovative consumers are adopting the product. In the maturity phase, the more cautious consumers buy the product, until finally another product comes along which has more benefits or which does a better job, and the consumers switch to the new product. The basic problem for marketers lies in knowing how long the maturity phase will last; this makes it difficult to use the product life cycle as a predictor of product obsolescence. It does tell us that all products eventually fade and die, and marketers should therefore develop new products to replace the old ones as these products fall out of favour with consumers.

Although we can be reasonably sure that all old products will eventually fail, we cannot by any means be sure that a new product will succeed. The lack of a good predictive system for forecasting product success wastes resources, since producers will spend time and effort making things that consumers do not want to buy. The ideal outcome for a producer is to develop products that become *culturally anchored* – that become part of modern life. Recent examples are the microwave oven, the video recorder and the personal computer – none of which would have been part of the average household twenty years ago, but which now would be difficult to manage without. In practice, such breakthroughs are hard to achieve. Understandably, with so much at stake for firms, there has been a great deal of research interest in innovation, with many researchers trying to determine what are the critical factors in new product success.

The process of adoption of innovation has much more to do with communication throughout the population than with individual decision making. Each individual will make decisions by the processes already outlined for existing products; the main difference is that there will be many fewer sources of information about an innovative product, since few people will have any experience of it as yet. Everett M. Rogers[13] postulated that products would be adopted if they possessed most of the attributes listed in Table 8.1.

Table 8.1 Product attributes necessary for adoption

Attribute	Explanation	Examples
Relative advantage	The product must have some advantage over the products already on the market. It must offer the consumer a better range of benefits than the existing solution, in other words.	Before the Sony Walkman was launched, the only way to listen to stereo-quality music was to carry a 'ghetto-blaster' on your shoulder. The Walkman replaced this cumbersome and anti-social device within a few years.
Compatibility	The product must fit in with the consumer's lifestyle.	At one time, the Welsh valleys had the highest rate of VCR ownership in the world. This was due to the high unemployment and lack of entertainment facilities in the area, making a video recorder a very convenient way of providing entertainment.
Complexity	The product must not be too complex for the consumer to understand.	Apple Mac scored a great success with user-friendly software with amusing and entertaining 'add-ons'. The company made serious inroads into IBM's market, despite being a very much smaller company.
Trialability	Products which can be tried out are more likely to succeed.	When Daewoo cars were launched in Britain, several thousand consumers were invited to test drive the car. Those who took up the offer were given free videos as an inducement.
Observability	The more observable the product, the quicker the diffusion process. If other potential consumers are able to see the product in use, this is bound to raise interest in it.	Part of the reason for the Walkman's worldwide success is that it can clearly be observed in use. Likewise, new fashion ideas seem to catch on very quickly; this is due to the high level of observability.

There have been several models of the adoption process, most of which assume a somewhat complex process of assessing the new product. In the case of radically new products (those which will alter the user's lifestyle) this may well be the case, but since most products which are classified as new are, in fact, adaptations of existing products, it might be safe to assume that the consumers do not necessarily carry out a lengthy evaluation of the type assumed by most researchers. Five adoption models are diagrammed in Figure 8.6.

The main feature that all these models have in common is that they show that innovations take a long time to be adopted. This means that it may be a year or more before a new product begins to show a return; this is implicit also in the shape of the product life cycle curve, where the introduction

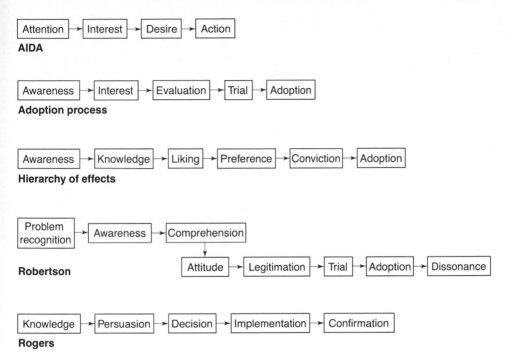

Figure 8.6 Models of the adoption and diffusion process (Sources: Robertson adapted from Thomas S. Robertson, 'The process of innovation and the diffusion of innovation', *Journal of Marketing*, vol. 31, January 1967, pp. 14–19; Rogers adapted from Everett M. Rogers, *Diffusion of Innovation*, 3rd edn, New York: Free Press, 1983)

phase shows a slow start. Often firms decide too early that a product is not succeeding, and take it off the market before consumers have completed the evaluation process.

A second focus in the research has been on the consumers most likely to buy new products: the *innovators*, in other words. The reason for this is that there is an assumption that innovation is diffused by word-of-mouth, or that innovators are likely to influence others to buy the products. This is implicit in the product life cycle, and in Rogers' observability criterion.

It is perfectly feasible to classify consumers in terms of their attitude to new products; the problem with identifying innovators is that they are not usually innovative in all their buying habits. That is to say, an innovator for hi-fi equipment is not necessarily an innovator for breakfast cereals, and although there is some evidence that there may be a kind of super-innovator who likes virtually everything that is new, these people are difficult to find, and it is debatable whether they are likely to influence other buyers anyway.[14]

Everett Rogers classified consumers as innovators (2.5 per cent of the population), early adopters (13.5 per cent), early majority (34 per cent), late majority (34 per cent), and laggards (16 per cent). These classifications were originally devised from agricultural product adoptions, but have been widely accepted as applying to consumers equally well. The percentages given are arbitrary; everybody is at some point along a continuum, and Rogers decided that those whose scores lay more than two standard deviations from the mean would be classed as innovators, those whose scores lay between one and two standard deviations would be the early majority, and so forth.

Innovativeness is the degree to which a person tends to adopt innovations earlier than other people. It can be measured very simply using the Goldsmith–Hofacker Innovativeness Scale, which uses six questions to determine an individual's innovativeness in respect to a particular product category.[15] The Goldsmith–Hofacker Scale is, in a sense, too simplistic because it merely asks what the individual's behaviour is, without finding out what it is about people that makes them into innovators. In order to try to discover what it is that makes somebody an innovator, studies have been carried out into known innovators to find out what they have in common. Three main groups of variable have been identified thus far: socioeconomic factors, personality factors and communication behaviour.[16] It should be noted, again, that all these studies are based on limited product categories, and are therefore not necessarily generally applicable.

Socioeconomic variables which are positively related to innovativeness are as follows:

- Education.
- Literacy.
- Higher social status.
- Upward social mobility.
- Larger-sized units.
- Commercial rather than subsistence orientation.
- More favourable attitude towards credit.
- More specialized operations.

Clearly, higher-income people are in a much better position to take the risk of buying new products. Those who are educated and literate are also more likely to hear about new products before other people do.

Personality and attitude variables associated with innovativeness are as follows:

- Empathy.
- Ability to deal with abstractions.

- Rationality.
- Intelligence.
- Favourable attitude towards change.
- Ability to cope with uncertainty.
- Favourable attitude towards education.
- Favourable attitude towards science.
- Achievement motivation.
- High aspirations.

However, there are some personality traits that militate against innovativeness:

- Dogmatism.
- Fatalism.

M.J. Kirton[17] showed that consumers can be classified as either adapters or innovators. Adapters tend to take existing solutions and adjust them as necessary to fit the current need problem; innovators tend to look for radical solutions. Kirton's Adaption–Innovation Index has proved to be a very reliable measure of innovativeness.

Cognitive innovators tend to be those who seek out new intellectual experiences, whereas *sensory innovators* are those who seek new sensory experiences. In both cases the innovators are seeking something new for its own sake; and there is ample research to indicate that novelty is an attractive feature of a product in its own right.

Communication variables that are positively associated with innovativeness are as follows:

- Social participation.
- Interconnectiveness with the social system.
- Cosmopolitanism.
- Change agent contact.
- Mass media exposure.
- Exposure to interpersonal communication channels.
- Knowledge of innovations.
- Opinion leadership.
- Belonging to highly interconnected systems.

Although innovators for one product group are not necessarily innovators for other groups, there are some correlations. For example, *technophiles* are people who like technology for its own sake, and who are prepared to take an interest in (and even buy) new computers, electronic gadgets, miniature TVs and so forth, whereas *technophobes* have a loathing for such devices. There is some evidence to suggest that technophiles are less likely to be innovators for fashion items and food products.[18] These studies are still in their early stages, however, since the subject area is extremely complex.

From the viewpoint of a marketer, it would appear that there is a demand for newness *per se*. In other words, as a general rule, people like new things and like to feel that the product they buy now is better than the one they bought ten years ago. On the other hand, consumers are not necessarily prepared to take the risk of buying products that are radically different from their existing purchases.

In terms of the effect on the consumer's lifestyle (and consequently the risk to the consumer), innovations can be classified under three headings:[19]

- *Continuous innovation*: a relatively minor change in the product, such as the packaging or the styling.
- *Dynamically continuous*: changes which materially affect the core functioning of the product, such as a rally version of a family saloon.
- *Discontinuous*: a product which is new to the world, and changes the lifestyles of those who adopt it, such as the microwave oven.

A study by Calentone and Cooper[20] found that the most successful new products were, in fact, only incremental improvements on existing products, rather than radically new products. This study also emphasized the need for the product to have a marketing synergy rather than to be simply a wonderful idea which the engineering department thought might succeed.

In this connection, the recent trend towards *benchmarking* is likely to lead to even more 'me-too' or incremental product offerings. Benchmarking is the process by which firms compare their activities with the best in the industry, and try to match the best practice of their competitors in each area. The aim is to become the best of the best. To this end, motor manufacturers buy their competitors' cars and strip them down to see how they are made and what their features are, then try to emulate the best of them in their own product offerings. Inevitably this will lead to more copying of competitors' products if the philosophy is applied to new product development.

Part of the problem for manufacturers is that there is no generally agreed definition of newness. For the purposes of marketing, manufacturers really have to rely on the consumer's perception of what is new and what is not.

Since this is very much a subjective and individualistic perception, the manufacturer frequently finds itself in a marketing minefield.

Marketing approaches to new product launches

Combining decision-making theory and diffusion theory, it is possible to come up with some broad recommendations for launching new products.

1. *Need recognition.* Marketers should activate the needs by mentioning them in advertising. The advertising needs to make people aware of what is new, and how it will have a *relative advantage* over current competitors.
2. *Pre-purchase activities or search.* Information sources are strongly linked to marketing strategy; brochures, product information adverts, leaflets, PR activities and salespeople all contribute to the process. Marketers should ensure that there is an emphasis on the product's *compatibility* with the target market's lifestyles and aspirations.
3. *Evaluation and purchase decision.* Salespeople have a strong contribution to make to this part of the process; marketers must ensure a high quality of presentation of information materials, and the sales force must be able to guide consumers through the *complexity* of the product.
4. *Act of purchase and consumption.* The product has to be right for the task, and fulfil the manufacturer's claims. Allowing the customer to try the product out is a good means of reducing the risk, so trialability is a key issue in this context.
5. *Post-purchase evaluation.* After-sales service has a strong role to play here, and ideally there should be some *observability* in the product if there is to be rapid diffusion of the product to the broader market.

Key points from this chapter

This chapter has been about consumer decision-making processes, and particularly about new product adoption. The key points are as follows:

- Needs become activated when there is a divergence between the actual and the desired states.
- Any information search is likely to be limited, since there is a cost attached as well as a risk-reduction aspect.

- The type of problem solving undertaken will depend in part on whether the consumer is replenishing the assortment or extending it.
- The consideration set does not include every possible solution.
- Most decisions involve decision rules, either pre-programmed or invented on the spot.
- Firms must innovate or die because the product life cycle ensures that all products eventually become obsolete.
- Innovators for one product category are not necessarily innovators for any other product category.
- The most successful products are often me-toos or continuous innovations.
- Launch and diffusion of new products takes time, so be patient!

Notes

1. John Dewey, *How We Think* (Boston, MA: D.C. Heath & Co., 1910).
2. Sak Onkvisit and John J. Shaw, *Consumer Behaviour, Strategy and Analysis* (New York: Macmillan, 1994), chapter 18.
3. Wayne D. Hoyer and Nancy M. Ridgway, 'Variety seeking as an explanation for exploratory purchase behaviour: a theoretical model', in Thomas C. Kinnear (ed.), *Advances in Consumer Research*, vol. 11, (Provo, UT: Association for Consumer Research, 1984).
4. Roger A. Formisan, Richard W. Olshavsky and Shelley Tapp, 'Choice strategy in a difficult task environment', *Journal of Consumer Research*, vol. 8 (March 1982), pp. 474–9.
5. Hawkins Stern, 'The significance of impulse buying today' *Journal of Marketing*, vol. 26 (April 1962), pp. 59–60.
6. James F. Bettman and C.W. Park, 'Effects of prior knowledge and experience and phase of choice processes on consumer decision processes: a protocol analysis', *Journal of Consumer Research*, vol. 7 (August 1980), pp. 234–48.
7. Geoffrey C. Kiel and Roger A. Layton, 'Dimensions of consumer information seeking behaviour', *Journal of Marketing Research*, vol. 18 (May 1981), pp. 233–9.
8. Raymond A. Bauer, 'Consumer behaviour as risk taking', in Robert S. Hancock (ed.), *Dynamic Marketing for a Changing World* (Chicago, IL: American Marketing Association, 1960).
9. Joel E.Urbany, 'An experimental examination of the economics of information', *Journal of Consumer Research*, vol. 13 (September 1986), pp. 257–71.
10. Peter H. Bloch, Daniel L. Sherrell and Nancy M. Ridgway, 'Consumer search: an extended framework', *Journal of Consumer Research*, vol. 13 (June 1986), pp. 119–26.
11. Louis P. Bucklin, 'Retail strategy and the classification of consumer goods', *Journal of Marketing*, vol. 27 (January 1963), pp. 50–4.

12. James R. Bettman, *An Information Processing Theory of Consumer Choice* (Reading, MA: Addison-Wesley, 1979), chapter 7.
13. Everett M. Rogers, *Diffusion of Innovation*, 3rd edn (New York: Free Press 1983).
14. John O. Summers, 'Generalised change agents and innovativeness', *Journal of Marketing Research*, vol. 8 (August 1971), pp. 313–16.
15. R.E. Goldsmith and C.F. Hofacker, 'Measuring consumer innovativeness', *Journal of the Academy of Marketing Science*, vol. 19, no. 3 (1991), pp. 209–22.
16. Rogers, *Diffusion of Innovation*, op cit.
17. 'Adapters and innovators: a theory of cognitive style', in K. Gronhaugh and M. Kaufman (eds.), *Innovation: A crossdisciplinary perspective* (New York: John Wiley, 1986).
18. James F. Engel, Roger D. Blackwell and Paul W. Miniard, *Consumer Behaviour*, 8th edn (Fort Worth, TX: Dryden Press, 1995), chapter 24.
19. Thomas S. Robertson, 'The process of innovation and the diffusion of innovation', *Journal of Marketing* (January 1967), pp. 14–19.
20. Roger J. Calentone and Robert G. Cooper, 'New product scenarios: prospects for success', *American Journal of Marketing*, vol. 45 (Spring 1981), pp. 48–60.

9

High-involvement purchasing behaviour

This chapter is about those purchases which carry the highest levels of emotion and commitment. High-involvement purchases, purchases of unsought goods, self-image purchasing and purchases of complex, high-tech goods all stretch the consumer's emotions and energy. After reading this chapter, you should be able to:

- Explain the role of involvement in consumer decision making.
- Describe how the sales function operates for unsought goods.
- Explain why consumers will not seek out products, even when there is a recognized need.
- Formulate strategies for launching high-value unsought goods.

Involvement

Involvement is the perceived importance or personal relevance of an object or event. It is about the degree to which the consumer feels attached to the product or brand, and the loyalty felt towards it. Involvement has both cognitive and affective elements: it plays on both the brain and the emotions. For example, a car owner might say, 'I love my VW Beetle [affect] because it never lets me down [cognition].'

High product involvement will come about if the consumer feels that product attributes are strongly-linked to *end goals* or *values*; lower levels of involvement occur if the attributes only link to *function*, and low levels occur if attributes are irrelevant to consequences.

High-involvement purchases are those products which figure greatly in the consumer's lifestyle. In other words, they involve decisions which it is

138

Table 9.1 Comparison of involvement levels

High involvement	Medium involvement	Low involvement
Attributes strongly linked to end goals	Attributes only link to function	Attributes irrelevant to consequences
Important to get it right first time	Need to have reasonably reliable results	Results perceived to be the same whichever product chosen
Consumer has in-depth knowledge and strong opinions	Consumer has knowledge of the product group, no strong feelings	No strong feelings, knowledge of product group irrelevant
Discrepant information ignored or discounted	Discrepant information considered carefully	Discrepant information ignored

important to get right, preferably first time. Typically, the products with which the consumer is highly involved will also be the ones which the consumer knows most about, and about which he or she has strong opinions.

Table 9.1 compares high-involvement, medium-involvement and low-involvement considerations. For example, a semi-professional musician might have very strong views on which guitar strings give the best sound and are easiest to play. He may become very loyal to Ernie Ball Super Slinkies and be prepared to scour the music shops to get them. Discrepant information (a salesperson's attempt to persuade him to try another brand, for example) is discounted and disparaged, and may even lower the esteem of the source of the information (the musician will think the salesperson is stupid, or is trying to unload an inferior brand of string). A beginner guitarist, on the other hand, is less likely to have formed a close involvement with a product in this way, and is more likely to be prepared to listen to what the salesperson has to say.

This means that high-involvement consumers are hard to persuade: they will not be easily swayed by advertising or even by persuasive sales pitches.[1] Here is another example.

In the spring of 1985, Coca-Cola announced that it was changing the formula of standard Coke. Most people preferred the new flavour in blind taste tests, and the original formula had not been changed in nearly a century, so the company felt justified in going ahead with the new product. Unfortunately, the company had not taken account of the degree of involvement Coke consumers had with the product. Most of them remembered Coke from their childhood, and had grown up with it; the product held emotional connotations (which had been fostered by the Coca-Cola Company in the past) and found the new formula unacceptable simply because it denoted the demise of the original Coke. Shortly after the launch of the new Coke, the company had to withdraw the changes and revert to the original formula after a wave of protest swept the world. Coke just wasn't Coke any more; people have a strong emotional attachment to it and did not like this being taken away.[2]

Levels of involvement are influenced by two sources: *personal sources* and *situational sources*. Personal sources (also called *intrinsic self-relevance*) are the means–end knowledge stored in the individual's memory, and are influenced both by the person and by the product. Consumers who believe that the attributes of the product link strongly to important end goals are likely to be more heavily involved with the product because the importance of the end goals mean that it is essential to get the product (the means to the end) right first time. For example, an individual who believes that wearing a smart suit to a job interview is a sure way of getting the job will take particular care in choosing a suit if the job is particularly desirable. Involvement does not necessarily rely on the outcomes being positive; sometimes involvement is greater if there might be negative consequences, since the consumer will take care to choose a product that will help to avoid an unpleasant outcome.

Since there is always a risk with any purchase behaviour, and high-involvement goods in particular are the ones that are most important to the consumer, consumers will usually engage in extended problem-solving behaviour when first purchasing high-involvement goods. Having taken the risk of choosing a brand, the highly involved individual will not want to switch brands later unless absolutely necessary (for example, if the favourite brand goes out of production). When brand switching becomes necessary, the consumer will again go through the extensive problem-solving routine.

Situational sources of involvement are concerned with aspects of the immediate social or physical surroundings of the consumer. Sometimes a change in *social circumstances* will increase involvement: most people give considerable thought to how they will dress when going on a first date, for example. *Physical environment* issues are about the circumstances that arise in the surrounding environment rather than those involving people. For example, a climber might revise her view of the importance of reliability if her climbing-rope were to fail halfway up a rock face. Likewise, experience of cold weather might cause an individual to become strongly involved with a ski jacket.

Figure 9.1 shows the relationship between the characteristics of consumers and products, and the routes by which these generate involvement and, ultimately, a purchase (or non-purchase) decision.

Marketers may be able to manipulate some of the environmental aspects in order to increase consumer involvement in some way. For instance, a salesperson might explain the possible consequences of buying the wrong type of double glazing (showing that not all double glazing has the same insulating qualities, for example). This may make the customer aware that

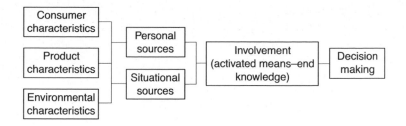

Figure 9.1 Relationship between consumer characteristics and product characteristics (Sources: Adapted from Richard L. Celsi and Jerry C. Olson, 'The role of involvement in attention and comprehension processes', *Journal of Consumer Research*, vol. 15, September 1988, pp. 210–24; Peter H. Bloch and Marsha L. Richins, 'A theoretical model for the study of product importance perceptions', *Journal of Marketing*, vol. 47, Summer 1983, pp. 69–81)

the end result (having paid out a lot of money for windows that do not keep the heat in) could be highly self-relevant.

Consumers frequently develop close relationships with brands and products. Examples are aftershave, perfumes, jeans, cars and cigarettes. Although most smokers cannot identify their favourite brand in blind taste tests, it would take considerable persuasion to make them switch brands; likewise, drivers develop affective relationships with their cars. A driver's first car is often given a nickname, and is personalized with stickers and add-ons. Drivers frequently talk to their cars, even asking them questions; this has been used to great effect in advertisements for the Renault Megane, where the car is heard to be talking back to the driver.

Consumers can be categorized according to their level of involvement, as Table 9.2 shows. The classifications, of course, will apply only to a particular product category. A consumer may be staunchly loyal to a brand of whisky, while not caring which brand of soda water goes in it. While it is undoubtedly true that some people will be heavily involved with a lot of different brands while others do not pay much attention to branding, there is no evidence that high involvement in one brand will lead to high involvement in another brand from a different product category.

Involvement does not always equate to price. A high-involvement good is not necessarily a high-priced one, nor is a low-involvement good necessarily a cheap one.[3] Smokers can become very involved with their brand of cigarettes, at only a few pounds a packet; beer drinkers become heavily involved in their favourite brand of beer, at only £2 a pint or less. Conversely, some people do not really care what car they drive, as long as it goes and gets them from A to B, or perhaps a computer owner might spend £3,000 on a machine simply because he or she has to work from home a lot, without feeling any particular love of the machine. In other words, there may be no affective element in the purchase.

Table 9.2 Categories of consumer according to involvement

Brand loyalists	Strong affective links to a favourite brand. Usually they tend to link the product category to the provision of personally relevant consequences. These are people who go for the 'best brand' for their needs, but also feel that the product category itself is an important part of their lives.
Routine brand buyers	Low personal sources of involvement, but have a favourite brand. These consumers are more interested in the types of consequence associated with regular brand purchases (it is easier to buy the same one each week, and it is at least reliable). They are not necessarily looking for the 'best brand'; a satisfactory one will do.
Information seekers	Have positive means–end information about the product category, but no one brand stands out as superior. They use a lot of information to help them find a suitable brand from within the product category.
Brand switchers	Low brand loyalty, low personal involvement. These people do not see that the brand used has any important consequences, even if the product category is interesting. Usually they do not have a strong relationship with the product category either. This means that they are easily affected by environmental factors such as sales promotions.

Source: J. Paul Peter and Jerry C. Olson, *Understanding Consumer Behaviour* (Burr Ridge, IL: Irwin, 1994).

High involvement always has a strong affective component, and this does not necessarily mean a high cost commitment. People also fall in love with cheap products!

Purchasing high-tech consumer durables

Consumer durables such as stereo equipment, cameras, video recorders and computers are frequently high-involvement purchases. This is because there is usually a high level of personal relevance when somebody is contemplating the purchase of an expensive and highly visible piece of equipment. This could be because of the social values applied (friends being envious or admiring), or perhaps because of a situational change. The consumer contemplating a high-tech purchase is likely to have acquired, or be acquiring, extensive means–end knowledge.

Factors in the decision-making framework might include the following:

- *Self-image considerations*. Does this piece of equipment fit into the kind of image the buyer has of him or herself, or the kind of image to be projected to others?

- *Situational sources of involvement*. Does this piece of equipment meet an immediate need? For example, a consumer might need to purchase a computer that will run software compatible with that used in work.
- *Product-related considerations*. How long will the equipment last? Consumer durables are usually bought only rarely – perhaps every seven or eight years or so, and therefore there is a strong incentive to buy products that will suit the purpose, since they will be around for a long time.
- *Information considerations*. Purchasers will probably be information seekers, since frequency of purchase is low, and the high-tech products change frequently. Personal sources of information are therefore likely to be obsolete.
- *Financial risk*. This is fairly high, since high-tech goods are usually expensive.
- *Social risk*. This can also be high, since high-tech goods are often bought by 'cognoscenti', whose friends and associates might be contemptuous of a poor purchase decision.
- Marketers can adopt a *rational, information-based* approach to promotion, since the purchasers are likely to be information seekers.

Typically, marketers of hi-fi equipment produce very detailed, highly technical brochures and information. Occasionally consumers criticise these, but many hi-fi owners not only understand all the jargon in the brochures, they welcome it as an indication of their membership of an élite group.

Unsought goods

So far, we have been looking at the consumer's behaviour when seeking out goods to meet a recognized need. While most goods fall into the category of being sought out as solutions to a need, there is a category of *unsought goods* which consumers do not go looking for.

Unsought goods are those goods for which consumers will recognize a need, but which they tend to avoid buying. Examples are double glazing (or indeed most home improvements), insurance, pensions and timeshare apartments.

If consumers do not seek out these products, two questions arise: first, why don't people seek them out when they have already recognized that there is a need; and second, how are such products marketed?

The possible reasons for not seeking out the products are as follows:

- Consumers do not like to think about the reasons for needing the products. For example, people do not like to think about old age and death, so they prefer not to think about insurance and pensions.

- The products are often expensive or require a long-term commitment, and consumers do not like to take the risk of making a mistake.
- There is usually no urgency about seeking a solution. The windows can last another year, or retirement is a long way off.
- The consumer may not see any immediate benefit. In the case of life insurance, the insured person *never* benefits directly, since the policy only pays out on proof of death.
- Some unsought goods are new on the market, so the level of knowledge about them is low and the consumer will automatically say 'Not interested'. Trust in both the product and the brand needs to be established first.

Marketers can overcome these problems with a series of tactics, but the main one is to use salespeople to explain the benefits of the product and close the sale. These salespeople usually have to overcome an initial resistance to the idea of spending time listening to a presentation, since the consumer of unsought goods is not engaged in an information search and is unprepared for spending any time or resources on it. The salesperson will therefore need to employ a tactical device to gain the customer's attention for long enough to activate the need for the product.

Insurance salespeople often do this by using the referred-name method. The salesperson will ask an existing customer (or a friend or acquaintance) for the name of somebody who might be interested in the product, and will then call up the person on the telephone and explain that a mutual acquaintance has recommended him or her. This reassures the recipient of the phone call and puts him or her under a certain amount of social pressure to hear the salesperson's story.

Table 9.3 shows some tactics for overcoming initial reluctance on the part of the consumer.

The next stage in the selling process is to activate the need. Here the salesperson must bring the problem to the forefront of the consumer's mind, and the consumer must recognize that something needs to be done about it. Having done this, it is possible to present a solution and 'save the day' for the consumer. Table 9.4 shows the sequence of selling a life insurance policy to a young couple, with the key phrases inserted. A presentation for life insurance is likely to take some time – over an hour and possibly a whole evening, depending on what problems are presented – so this table shows only the very basic outline.

Unsought goods highlight the difference between *want* and *need*. As we saw earlier, a need is a perceived lack, whereas a want is a specific satisfier. For unsought goods, the need is not there because it is unperceived. On the occasions when the consumer does perceive the lack of, say, life insurance, the thought of death usually causes the individual to put the thought of insurance out of his or her mind immediately. The salesperson's job is to

Table 9.3 Tactics for overcoming sales resistance

Tactic	Explanation
Provide a small free gift in exchange for hearing a presentation, or having a quotation. Often used by insurance companies and timeshare salespeople.	This compensates the consumer for what he or she thinks of as a waste of time. Also accepting the gift puts the consumer under a moral obligation to hear the salesperson out.
Make an appointment for the presentation, and give some literature. Often used for home-improvement sales where appointments are made on the door.	This prepares the consumer for the information search procedure. The literature is there to whet the consumer's appetite and activate the need.
Ensure that all decision-makers are present. Used in virtually all home-improvement selling.	This ensures that there is no need to repeat information or waste the consumer's time calling back.
Seek recommendations from each customer for other people to contact. Often used in insurance.	Reassures the consumer that the salesperson is reputable.

activate that need, to bring it to the forefront of the consumer's mind and keep it there long enough to present the solution. Since the consumer really does not want to have to keep thinking about these unpleasant things, he or she is unlikely to do much shopping around following the salesperson's visit. For this reason the bulk of unsought goods are sold on the first or second visit.

Because salespeople have felt compelled to use various closing techniques to get consumers to make decisions in difficult areas, consumer groups and others have raised objections to what are seen as high-pressure techniques. This has, in turn, led to legislation allowing consumers cooling-off periods of a few days during which they can cancel the agreements without penalty. Often consumers will have second thoughts, and often these second thoughts are based more on a fear of commitment than on any reasoned objection to the product. This is called *buyer's remorse*.

When a new invention first appears on the market, it is likely to be an unsought good, particularly if it is expensive. Double glazing first appeared in the UK in the 1960s, at which time people had not heard of it, and so naturally would not know to seek it out. Since the product was new, there were no existing owners, so there was no opportunity for people to observe it in use or to try out the advantages. Double glazing is almost always tailor-made to fit the specific house; it therefore has no second-hand value and there is no going back once it is fitted. This raises the risk level greatly for the consumer, and since the home is frequently a high-involvement good, the risk is even greater. As the market has matured and the majority of homes have at least some double glazing, consumers have had more chance to see the benefits. Many people have lived in houses with double

Table 9.4 Examples of the selling sequence

Stage of presentation	Salesperson's tactic	Consumer response	Explanation
Prospecting	'I was talking to Frank Jones, and he said that you might be able to benefit from some of our products. Frank suggested I come and see you – would Thursday evening be OK?'	Since Frank Jones is a friend, the customer is somewhat reassured and makes the appointment.	Social pressure overcomes the initial reluctance to talk to a salesperson; after all, the consumer does not have to buy anything.
Ice-breaking	'This is a nice area. Have you lived here long? We thought of moving up here at one time ourselves.'	The consumer feels that this salesperson is, after all, a human being with similar wants/needs to the consumer.	The purpose of ice breaking is to remove the adversarial connotations of a salesperson trying to get money off a customer, and show the salesperson as really being an adviser.
Needs identification	The salesperson asks a series of open questions designed to find out what the customer's needs are. For example, a pension salesman might ask 'How much money do you think you'll need to live on when you retire?'	The consumer will begin to think 'Yes, I do need to do something about this.' The need has become *activated* in the consumer's mind.	The consumer accepts that the needs exist because he has told the salesman; this would not be the case if the salesman did the telling.
Summarizing needs	The salesperson lists the needs to check that both parties understand where the consumer's problem lies.	'I didn't realize there were so many problems.'	This generates an atmosphere of urgency in the consumer's mind; there is now a need actually to do something about the problems. The consumer is now prepared to listen to the solution that the salesperson is about to propose.

The solution	The salesperson presents a solution, tailored to and phrased for the list of needs identified earlier.	'That sounds as if it will fit the case.'	The consumer is prepared to accept and understand the solution, having realized that something has 'to be done about the needs.
The close	The salesperson uses a phrase or technique to get the consumer to commit to the product: for example, the salesperson might say, 'Does that sound like it might work for you? Yes? Fine, we'll get the paperwork under way immediately. Could you just OK this for me?'	The consumer will often balk at making the final decision, simply because it is often a major commitment which is being considered.	The most difficult part of selling is to get a decision. Most closing techniques are designed to make it easy and natural for the customer to make a decision (preferably a yes decision).
Cementing the sale	The salesperson will make sure the customer is quite happy with everything, perhaps talking for a minute or two about the delivery time or the next stage of the purchase, or perhaps discussing something unrelated to the sale so as to avoid rushing off as soon as the order is signed.	The customer usually feels reassured and more confident that the decision has been a correct one.	There is a great deal more to selling and buying than mere economics. Particularly in the purchase of unsought goods there is a widespread distrust of salespeople, and the salesperson must therefore (a) break the ice carefully on arrival, and (b) leave the customer able to say, 'Look what I bought' rather than 'Look what I was sold'.

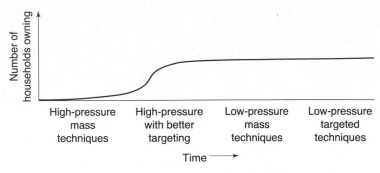

Techniques used for marketing the product category

Figure 9.2 Product maturity and the marketing approach

glazing and will have it fitted in new houses. Householders are now able to make reasonable comparisons between different types and brands of window, and this has led to a maturing of the market and a lessening of the need for salespeople to canvass.

A similar effect has occurred in the timeshare market in the USA, and in the solar heating market in Greece. Over a period of time, novel products which are also highly priced are likely to move from being unsought goods to being sought goods. This is shown diagrammatically in Figure 9.2.

When the product is first introduced, the industry marketing norm is to carry out a blanket approach, calling on every home without making any judgement as to which might be the most appropriate for the product. At this stage the salesperson will need to use 'high-pressure' techniques, first, to persuade the householder to hear about the product (information search) and, second, to persuade the householder to make a purchase decision. As the product becomes better established, market research can be undertaken to find out who are likely to be the best customers for the product, and the sales effort can be targeted in some ways. The technique will still involve fairly high pressure.

Once the product category is widely known, it is possible to use low-pressure techniques (for example, advertising '7 windows and a door, £1,100'). Even further down the line, it is possible to identify segments in the market and to advertise accordingly. For example, Pilkington's K Glass has a special coating to reflect heat back into the room, but since the coating would rub off if it were used in ordinary windows, it can only be specified for double glazing. This means that there must be a well-established double-glazing industry for the product to be viable. The insurance industry is now so well established that it is able to offer special deals to various occupational categories.

Table 9.5 Decision-making model for unsought goods

Stage	Techniques for management
Need recognition	Sales representative activates the need by asking questions.
Information search	Sales representative performs lengthy presentation, answering questions and objections as they arise.
Evaluation of alternatives	Salesperson *no-sells* the competition by pointing out where their products are inferior.
Choice decision	The close: some phrase or technique to obtain a decision.
Purchase	Complete the paperwork and cement the sale.
Post-purchase evaluation	Documentation sent by the company, follow-up visit by the salesperson. In the case of buyers' remorse, a return visit by the salesperson or sales manager.

Unsought goods present a problem to the marketer, in that they do not at first appear to fit the norms of consumer behaviour. On closer examination, though, it can be seen that the consumer goes through all the stages of purchase behaviour, with the difference that the process is managed almost entirely by the marketers. Table 9.5 illustrates this.

The selling techniques for unsought goods have attracted much adverse publicity, but it is worth bearing in mind that the vast majority of double-glazing owners are perfectly happy with the product; as are the vast majority of timeshare owners, and the vast majority of life insurance owners. Generally speaking, consumers are not stupid enough to commit large amounts of money to products they do not want and do not see a need for.

Key points from this chapter

This chapter has been about high-involvement and high-value purchasing behaviour. We have seen how risk avoidance and affect cause extended decision-making processes for these products, and how marketers can manage the process more thoroughly in the case of unsought goods.

Here are the key points from the chapter:

- Involvement is about the importance of the decision to the consumer.
- There are two sources of involvement – personal and situational.
- Situational sources of involvement are easier to influence than personal sources.
- Involvement is both cognitive and affective, but not necessarily in that order.

- High-involvement consumers are difficult to persuade.
- Involvement is tied up closely with self-esteem and self-image.
- High involvement does not necessarily relate to high cost.
- Purchase of unsought goods relies on strong process management by marketers.
- High-tech purchases are not necessarily high-involvement purchases.
- Affect plays a stronger role than cognition in high-involvement purchases.

Notes

1. C.A. Keisler, B.E. Collins and Norman Miller, *Attitude Change: A critical analysis of theoretical approaches* (New York: John Wiley, 1969).
2. Anne B. Fisher, 'Coke's brand-loyalty lesson', *Fortune*, August 1985.
3. Brian Beharrell and Tim J. Denison; 'Involvement in a routine food shopping context', *Proceedings of the MEG Annual Conference*, Ulster, 1994.

10

Segmentation

Segmentation is concerned with grouping consumers who have similar needs. This chapter is about ways in which this is done, and methods of assessing whether segments are economically worth pursuing.

After reading this chapter, you should be able to:

- Describe some of the main forms of segmenting markets.
- Explain the purpose of segmentation.
- Develop ways of assessing the economic viability of segments.
- Explain the growth of segmented markets.
- Establish strategies for dealing with segmented markets.

Reasons for segmenting markets

Market segmentation is the process of identifying a group of consumers with similar needs and producing a product that will meet those needs at a profit. It has a simple basis in logic: it is that no single product will appeal to all consumers.

Before the advent of mass production, there was a pent-up demand for basic, simple products, and this is still the case in some parts of the world, such as eastern Europe and the Third World. This meant that manufacturers could produce standardized products using long production runs to keep costs (and prices) as low as possible. In these circumstances, *undifferentiated marketing* approaches work well because people are prepared to put up with standardized goods and lack of choice rather than do without. Costs of mass production are so much less than the costs of hand production that

151

the prices can undercut anything custom-made, so that if the only choice is between one type of mass-produced article and a much more expensive hand-made version, consumers are often prepared to accept a product that is less than perfect for their needs.

For example, consider the manufacture of clothing. Prior to the industrial revolution most cloth was woven at home, or by hand in small factories. Clothing would be made to measure by tailors, and most people would perhaps only own one change of clothing, since the work involved in making each item by hand made the price high in comparison to people's earnings. With the advent of steam-powered looms, sewing machines and production lines, the cost of producing clothing fell to around one-tenth of the hand-made price. Although the new clothing was made to standard sizes, the cost was so much lower that people could own several changes of clothing, even if this meant putting up with a less than perfect fit. Even when British manufacturers had virtually eliminated competition from hand-loom producers, the rest of the world had yet to industrialize and so there was virtually no competition in export markets.

This led to the development of *mass markets* and firms using the *production orientation*. Under these conditions, the way to succeed in business was to ensure that the production costs (and hence the prices) were kept as low as possible. The greater the number of people who would buy the product, the greater the standardization and the longer the production run, so the greater the profits.

Clearly this approach works very well during times when choices are limited, and when production cannot keep up with demand. In First World countries in the late twentieth century, this approach is no longer viable because machine manufacturing is now so widespread that there is almost always another company elsewhere in the world with even lower production costs. Mass marketing still works in countries where there is very little outside competition (for example, the former Soviet Bloc countries, and some Third World countries where imports are severely restricted), but for most purposes it is true to say that there are very few mass markets left in western industrialized countries.

Undifferentiated marketing is less effective than segmented marketing in economies where most consumers already own the core benefits of the product. In other words, if most families already own a TV set, they have the core benefits of being able to receive TV programmes. Each family will have other needs: perhaps for teletext, or VCR functions, or stereo sound. Segmentation deals with finding out how many people are likely to want each benefit, roughly how much they will be willing to pay for it, and where they would like to buy it from. In this way, the firm approaching a segmented market is able to offer more functional benefits and more attention to hedonic needs: that is, the products are more fun.

Table 10.1 Development of transportation

Product type	Core benefits	Other benefits and drawbacks
Horse and carriage	Basic transportation for owner, passengers and goods	Easy to maintain, but unreliable, slow, not suitable for long-distance travel and expensive. Could be tailor-made for the individual owner. Only the most prosperous people could afford one.
Model T Ford	Basic transportation for owner, passengers and goods	Faster, more reliable, expensive. Standard engine, seating, colour ('Any colour you want as long as it's black') and components, so servicing is cheap.
Modern Ford vehicle range	Basic transportation for owner, passengers and goods	Reliable, cheap to buy and run, easy to maintain, fast and suitable for long-distance travel. Available in several hundred different combinations of body versions and engine sizes, according to individual preference, with a wide range of payment options to make it easy to buy. Optional extras include everything from wind spoilers to upgrade in radio equipment.

In large markets such as the USA (240 million consumers), the European Union (370 million consumers) and Japan (140 million consumers), there are often enough consumers with a specific need in common for manufacturers to be able to obtain the economies of scale enjoyed by British manufacturers in the mid-nineteenth century. Marketers now are able to treat consumers more as individuals, with individual wants and needs; in most industries we are not yet at the point where we can provide individual attention for individual consumers, so we need to identify groups of people with similar interests and design our approach to fit these groups. This is what segmentation seeks to achieve.

Table 10.1 shows how a basic product has gone through a series of changes over the course of a hundred years or so. Although people were prepared to buy the Model T Ford in huge numbers when it first appeared, it quickly became apparent that it was not fitting consumers' needs. This was evidenced by the fact that consumers were taking the basic model and adapting it themselves to suit their individual needs – cutting off the body and replacing it with a truck bed, altering the engine by drilling out the cylinders to make it more powerful, adding windows or removing the roof. It quickly became obvious to the Ford Motor Company that it could make more money by offering these alterations as factory alternatives and charging the customers a little more for them. Since this still worked out cheaper than doing the alterations themselves, customers were prepared to pay the extra money. Looked at from another angle, the options offered by the company made the product more desirable and therefore increased sales, despite the extra cost to the consumer.

The end result of this process is the modern range of Ford cars, which continually adapt in order to compete with other manufacturers which are carrying out a similar process of continual adaptation in response to consumer needs. The manufacturers' orientation has shifted from trying to produce cars as cheaply as possible towards trying to produce cars that are as desirable as possible.

Consumers are usually prepared to pay a premium price for a product that fits their needs more closely. This is because the cost–benefit relationship is more favourable if the benefits are much greater. By tailoring the products more nearly to consumers' needs, manufacturers are able to charge a little more, thus offsetting the extra costs of producing non-standardized products, and actually increasing profits as well.

Segmentation is an essential precursor to most marketing activities. Identifying a target group and knowing their needs allows us to *position* the product correctly in the target group's minds, and to adopt an appropriate *promotional strategy*, designing ads that appeal to the particular group. A well-known example of this is the Johnson's Baby products campaign. Johnson's became aware that more baby lotion and talcum powder was being sold than could be accounted for by the number of babies in the country; research showed that mothers were using the products on their own skins, believing that the products would be less harmful than those made for adults. This knowledge led Johnson's to reposition the products as an adult range, using the slogan 'Are you still a Johnson's baby?'

If we know where our target group shop, we can develop a *distribution strategy*, and knowing what the segment think of as good value will dictate our *pricing strategy*.

One of the most exciting developments in segmentation in recent years has been in the growth of *database marketing*, in which details of the consumer's purchases, lifestyle and behaviour can be used to tailor the marketing approach exactly, potentially to a 'segment of one'.[1] The foundation of database marketing is the increasing propensity of marketers to hold information about their customers on computer files. In some cases this information is very detailed: EPOS and EFTPOS systems in supermarkets hold details of every grocery purchase made by the consumer, and with the increasing use of loyalty cards the supermarkets can identify which consumers buy which combination of products.

Increased computing capability gives (at least theoretically) the ability to combine the records of databases held by different marketers, each of which hold information about the purchases of individual consumers, so as to provide a more complete picture of each person's behaviour and characteristics. The resulting database could hold, under each consumer's name and address, an almost complete picture of the consumer's purchasing behaviour. If information from credit card companies and bank computer files could be added, the consumer's income and expenditure could be defined exactly. It may even be possible, eventually, to anticipate an individual consumer's needs and make a direct approach with a solution for those needs.[2]

The aim of segmentation is to form a mental picture of the organization's ideal customer, and to plan everything around that person. In order to do this, the organization must be able to judge the size of the segment so as to form an opinion as to whether it is worthwhile producing a specialist product just for those people. Segments vary in size according to the following criteria:

- *Narrowness of definition of need.* For example, there may be a segment who prefer the product in blue, but this can subdivide further into metallic blue, dark blue, sky blue, etc. The narrower the definition, the smaller the segment.

- *Complexity of the product in terms of features available.* The more features a product has, the more segments it will appeal to and therefore the smaller the individual segments.

- *Consumer involvement with the product category.* If the product category generally attracts high-involvement consumers, the segments are likely to be small and loyal.

Clearly, the bigger the segment, the greater the profit potential as the benefits of standardisation and long production runs will be greater. On the other hand, the consumer's satisfaction with the product is likely to be less, as Figure 10.1 illustrates. The production run gets smaller as the product becomes more customized, but the customer satisfaction gets greater; a

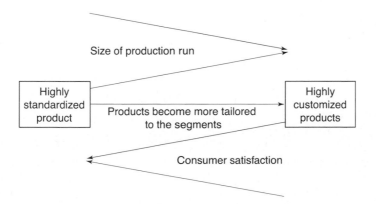

Figure 10.1 Segmentation trade-off

highly standardised product is cheaper to produce, but really pleases nobody.

Segmentation increases *profitability* when the value to the consumer of the improvements is greater than the cost to the manufacturer of providing them. This is because the manufacturer is able to charge a price higher than the cost of making the changes, but still less than it would cost the consumer to make adaptations after purchase.

For comparison, it is possible to buy clothes from a chain store that almost fit, and then take them home and alter the seams slightly so that the fit is perfect. It might be worthwhile, however, to pay a little extra at a different shop to buy something that already fits perfectly. This is the basis of the new Classic Combination catalogue. The catalogue company has measured 50,000 women and discovered that the shape of women's bodies has altered since the 1950s when the current standard dress sizes were fixed. The catalogue has taken this into account and re-tailored the clothes to fit the new body shapes.

Markets can be segmented according to many different factors: in the above example, the catalogue company will segment according to dress size as a matter of course, and will have carried out research to find out how many of each size it is likely to sell so that it can order the appropriate quantities. Apart from that, though, the company will also be segmenting according to consumer preference for dress styles, and this is a rather more complicated exercise.

The clothing market could be segmented *demographically* (according to age, income, family size, occupation, etc.), *psychographically* (according to behaviour patterns, attitudes, expectations), *geographically* (according to the area in which the people live, which may be relevant to a catalogue company, since more northerly customers will need warmer clothing), or even *behaviourally* (perhaps according to whether they already buy from other catalogues).

Suppose, for example, the company segments demographically. This may mean aiming the catalogue at a particular age group (perhaps 25 to 35-year-olds) or a particular income group, or perhaps both. If the company segments behaviourally, it may decide to aim at party-lovers and produce a lot of disco/party wear. (Some catalogues specialize in outdoor wear, for the hikers and mountaineers; others specialize in smart business wear for the career person).

A mail-order company is likely to be particularly interested in using database marketing, since this enables the company to send only those mailings which will interest the consumer they are aimed at. This will substantially cut the costs of sending out 'junk mail', since only those mailings of direct interest will be sent, and also the response rate from mailings should increase with more accurate targeting.

There are many other ways of segmenting markets, but all the methods serve the same function: they allow the company to specialize in what it can do best, and spend its marketing budget in the most effective way rather than spreading it too thinly by trying to please everybody.

Choosing a segment

For a segment to be viable, it must have the following characteristics:

- *Measurability*. It must be possible to find out how many people there are in the segment, and where they are, otherwise there is no way of knowing how big the market is going to be.
- *Accessibility*. It must be possible to approach them in some identifiable way. For instance, if it is a geographical segment, is there a retailer in the area which would carry our product? If the segment is defined in terms of behaviour (say, golfers), is there a suitable magazine to advertise in?
- *Substantiality*. Is the segment big enough to be economically worthwhile? This is a complex issue because it is not just a matter of saying whether there are enough people in the segment to make a viable market. There is also the question of whether their needs are sufficiently unmet by their existing products for them to be prepared to pay a little more for our product.
- *Congruity*. The needs of the target group must be similar, otherwise our product will meet with the same problems as the existing one; it will not meet everybody's needs well enough.

What firms are looking for is a group of people whose needs are not being met, and who are prepared to pay extra (a premium price) for a product that will meet those needs better than the product they are currently using. The equation for determining the viability of a segment is the number of people in the segment multiplied by the premium they are prepared to pay.

Firms can make good profits from a few people who are prepared to pay a lot extra to get exactly what they want, or from a lot of people who are prepared to pay a little extra to get what they want. The most profitable segments, of course, are those which have many members who are prepared to pay a high extra premium for the benefits of a product which more exactly meets their needs. Note that the product must meet the consumers' needs sufficiently better to remain good value for money.

The computer billionaires such as Bill Gates of Microsoft follow exactly this approach. The production cost of software is huge in terms of setting-up costs; writing new software takes many hours of highly skilled (and highly paid) work. Once the software is written, though, the cost of putting it on to diskettes is tiny by comparison: a blank diskette costing 10p to produce is worth £90 or more to the consumer once the software is on it. Consider the advent of desktop publishing. Before DTP, anybody wanting to produce camera-ready artwork, or produce a small newsletter with attractive typefaces and illustrations, would have to pay a graphic artist and a printer several hundred pounds to produce the work. With DTP, the consumer can do most of this work at home or in the office. Consumers are therefore prepared to pay £90 for the software because it will save them hundreds of pounds in wasted time and fees to printers.

What Bill Gates of Microsoft has managed to achieve is to tap into a market where there are literally hundreds of millions of people all over the world using his software, paying big premiums to do so because the previous solutions (typewriting, paying printers, etc.) were very cumbersome and expensive, and the net production cost, while high in absolute terms, is low when spread over the size of market the software has.

Segmenting a market

It is important when segmenting a market not to use arbitrary assumptions, but there is often no simple way to determine the best way to segment. The first decision will be to determine the basis of the segmentation, whether demographically, geographically, behaviourally or psychographically. Within these bases there will be subdivisions, as Table 10.2 illustrates.

Geographic segmentation may be carried out for a number of reasons. First, the nature of the product may be such that it really only applies to people living in a specific area, or type of area. There is really no point in trying to sell air-conditioning to Eskimos when there is a ready market among Spaniards. (In fact the old story about the salesman who could sell sand to the Arabs only shows that the salesman in question had not heard of segmentation!) The market may also be segmented geographically if the company's resources are limited, so the firm starts out in a small area and later rolls out the product nationally. A third reason might be that the product itself does not travel well. This is true of sheet glass, wedding cakes and most personal services like hairdressing.

Because geography is often more relevant than age, the ACORN classifications are widely used. ACORN stands for A Classification Of Residential Neighbourhoods, and seeks to group consumers according to the type of housing they live in: in other words, by geographical area. Some of the groupings are given in Table 10.3. Because it is assumed that people choose where they live (within the limits of income) it appears that the ACORN classifications are better predictors of behaviour than socioeconomic

Table 10.2 Segmentation bases and subdivisions

Segmentation types or bases	Examples
Geographic segmentation	
Region	Scotland, north of England, south-east England, West Country, Wales
City size	Up to 100,000; 100,000 to 500,000; 500,000 to 1m; 1m +
Population density	Urban, suburban, rural
Climate	Warm, cold
Demographic segmentation	
Age	<12, 13–19, 20–39, 40–59, 60+
Gender	Female, male
Household size	1, 2, 3, 4, 5 or more
Income	Up to £10k per annum; £10,001 to £15k, £15,001 to £25k, £25k+
Occupation	Professional, blue-collar, retired, unemployed
Education	GCSE, A-level, college, university
Sociocultural segmentation	
Culture	European, Asian, African, Caribbean
Subculture: religion	Catholic, Jewish, Islamic, Protestant
Subculture: national origin	British, Indian, Chinese, Sudanese, Jamaican, etc.
Subculture: race	Asian, Caucasian, Afro-Caribbean
Social class	Aristocracy, upper class, middle class, working class
Marital status	Single, married, divorced, widowed, cohabiting
Psychographics	Achievers, strivers, strugglers.
Affective and cognitive segmentation	
Degree of knowledge	Expert, novice
Benefits sought	Convenience, economy, prestige
Attitude	Positive, neutral, negative
Behavioural segmentation	
Brand loyalty	None, divided, undivided loyalty
Store loyalty	None, divided, undivided loyalty
Usage rate	Light, medium, heavy
User status	Non-user, ex-user, current user, potential user
Payment method	Cash, credit, HP
Media usage	Newspapers, magazines, TV
Usage situation	Work, home, on holiday

Source: Adapted from J. Paul Peter and Jerry C. Olson, *Understanding Consumer Behaviour* (Burr Ridge, IL: Irwin, 1994), chapter 3.

groupings. In any event, ACORN is clearly of direct use when segmenting markets for home improvements or retail shop location.

Psychographic segmentation has the drawback that it is difficult to measure consumers' psychological attributes on a large scale. This means that this type of segmentation often fails on the grounds of accessibility. For example, the market research may have shown that there are a substantial number of consumers who are afraid of having their pets stolen for medical

Table 10.3 ACORN classifications

Categories	% of population	Groups	% of population
A. Thriving	19.8	1. Wealthy achievers, suburban areas	15.1
		2. Affluent greys, rural communities	2.3
		3. Prosperous pensioners, retirement areas	2.4
B. Expanding	11.6	4. Affluent executives, family areas	3.8
		5. Well-off workers, family areas	7.8
C. Rising	7.8	6. Affluent urbanites, town and city areas	2.3
		7. Prosperous professionals, metropolitan areas	2.1
		8. Better-off executives, inner-city areas	3.4
D. Settling	24.0	9. Comfortable middle-agers, mature home-owning areas	13.4
		10. Skilled workers, home-owning areas	10.6
E. Aspiring	13.7	11. New home-owners, mature communities	9.7
		12. White-collar workers, better-off multi-ethnic areas	4.0
F. Striving	22.6	13. Older people, less prosperous areas	3.6
		14. Council estate residents, better-off homes	11.5
		15. Council estate residents, high unemployment	2.7
		16. Council estate residents, greatest hardship	2.7
		17. People in multi-ethnic low-income areas	2.2
Unclassified	0.5		0.5

experiments. The problem now is that there is no obvious medium to advertise our new security system for pets in: if there were a magazine called *Pet Security Monthly*, we would have no problem. We are therefore left with the mass media, such as TV advertising, which is probably far too expensive for the purpose. Some of the most creative ideas in marketing have revolved around ways of gaining access to such segments.

Behaviour can be a useful and reliable way of segmenting. At its most obvious, if we are marketing to anglers, we are not interested in how old they are, what their views are on strong drink, or where they live. All we care about is that they go fishing, and might therefore be customers for our new type of rod. Accessing the segment would be easily undertaken by advertising in the *Angler's Times*. At a deeper level, we might be interested in such issues as where they buy their fishing tackle, how much they usually spend on a rod and what kind of fish they are after, but this information is easily obtained through questionnaire-type surveys.

Demographic segmentation is the most commonly used method of segmenting markets. Demographics is the study of the 'shape' of the population, and is concerned with areas such as age, occupation, salary and lifestyle stage.

The argument in favour of using demography as a segmentation variable is that people are the foundation of marketing analysis. We therefore need to ask ourselves:

- How many are there/will there be?
- What is/will be the age distribution?
- Where do/will they live?
- How long do they/will they live?

Population trends are fairly reliable statistically: we can predict how many 40-year-olds there will be in ten years' time because we know how many 30-year-olds we have now, and we know fairly accurately what the death rate is for people in their thirties. Even natural disasters, wars, plagues, etc. may not affect the figures too much, depending on the scope of the study. The biggest variable is likely to be births rather than deaths; of the three variables (births, deaths and immigration), births is the most volatile.

The number of births is dependent on several factors. *Birth rate* is the number of live births per thousand population in a given year. *Fertility rate* is the number of live births per thousand women of child-bearing age. *Completed fertility rate* is the total number ever born to women of a specific age group (an indication of family size). *Total fertility rate* (TFR) is the number of children a woman would expect to have in her lifetime if she passed through all the average completed fertility rates. This is a complex concept, but it gives an idea of how many children women are currently having. The current TFR is less than 1.8 for the UK; 2.1 will maintain the population, so if we were relying on births to replace people who die, the population would be falling. TFR is not to be confused with *natural increase*, which is the surplus of births over deaths, or *growth rate*, which includes migration effects.

The population of the European Union is increasing at present, but natural increase is actually negative. The difference is being made up by immigration, which means that there will be ethnic and cultural shifts in the population. There are ethnic differences in fertility rates and birth rates and this is also affecting the mix of population; partly these differences are cultural, because some cultures have a strong imperative towards large families, and partly they arise because migrants are predominantly of child-bearing age, but often have not yet started their families. Clearly once a couple have children it becomes much more difficult to switch countries. This again is leading to substantial cultural shifts within the host countries.

There are four variables in the birth rate: age, family structure, social attitudes and technology. *Age distribution* of the population affects birth rate, since an ageing population is likely to have fewer children per thousand than a younger population.

Family structure concerns areas such as marriages, women's employment outside the home, and the average age at first marriage. As more women are following careers, they are postponing having children (or even dropping the idea altogether) and therefore tending to have fewer of them. Fewer people are marrying now than previously, and many are marrying much later, so that the one-child family is becoming far more common.

Social attitudes towards issues such as illegitimacy have relaxed. Marriage and family are emphasized less nowadays, and there is a far weaker cultural imperative to reproduce. Even 30 years ago couples were under great pressure from their families and friends to have babies; nowadays the pressures are less, even when the prospective grandparents are eager for the couple to 'get started'.

Technology is mostly about the availability of contraception. As contraceptive techniques have improved, the birth rate has fallen because more people have been able to exercise choice in reproduction. This is not true in every country in the world: in Third World countries contraception is not widely available and therefore the birth rate remains high.

It is possible to identify shifts in attitude and behaviour that have come about due to rises and falls in the national birth rate.

The *baby boomers* were born in the fifteen years or so after the Second World War. This was a time of rising prosperity, when returning soldiers (and war-weary civilians) felt confident about starting families. The baby boomers are now aged around 35–50. Born and brought up in periods of rising prosperity, increasing personal freedom and rising expectations, they tend to pay cash for their purchases (although they used to use credit, interest rates are deterring them now they are richer). They tend to buy more and save less than previous generations, and banks will make less on providing them with credit over the next few years, but more on providing pensions and savings schemes.

Baby busters were born between 1964 and 1980 – a time of falling birth rates. There were also falling standards of living, oil crises, more social dislocation caused by the rise in one-parent and both-parents-working families. Baby busters tend to be heavy consumers, hard workers, educated, ambitious, selfish and determined to succeed financially. These are the generation that produced the yuppie.[3]

Woopies are well-off older people. Not all the over-65s are living in poverty; many have generous occupational pensions, low outgoings and substantial savings and investments. They spend more than the average on holidays, their homes and financial services. Many retired teachers, engineers, doctors and middle managers are in this position, and they now form a substantial market. Companies such as Saga Holidays have tapped into this market very successfully by providing holidays that are specifically tailored for elderly people: for example, Saga ensures that its clients rarely (if ever) have to carry their own luggage any distance, since elderly people might have difficulty with this. Saga holidays are not cheaper than others; they simply cater for the over-55s.

The population is ageing rapidly, due to two factors: falling birth rate and increased longevity. Between 1990 and 2000 the population of the European Union aged over 90 is expected to increase by 50 per cent at least. This has several effects:[4]

- Relationship marketing is more important if the relationship between company and consumer might last 50 years or more.
- More leisure time per head of population means more spending on leisure pursuits.
- The possibility of living to be very old may encourage younger people to look after themselves better, so there may be an upsurge in sales of health and fitness products.
- Fewer new consumers makes it important for marketers to look after the old ones better.

Marketers are facing new challenges from the shifting demography, not least the problem of zero population growth, which in theory means static or even shrinking markets. This inevitably means that marketers can no longer rely on the natural increase of the population to expand the company's business. They must instead be able to compete better for the consumer's money.

The segmentation bases described above are not necessarily mutually exclusive; it is perfectly feasible to aim for 20–30-year-old-men of Asian race who are expert motor mechanics and live in towns of less than 100,000 population. This would use demographic, sociocultural, geographic and cognitive segmentation. Naturally the number of men fitting into this category would be small, but (presumably) if such a segment were to have very similar needs, their level of interest in a product that would meet those needs would be correspondingly high.

Generally speaking, the narrower the segment, the more loyal and interested the consumers will be, but the fewer of them there are. Marketers therefore have to make strategic decisions about which segment should be approached.

Strategic options

Having segmented the market, there are three basic strategic options open to marketers. In reality, these are points on a continuum; segmentation is not exact, and therefore targeting a segment will not be an exact process.

- *Concentrated* marketing (single segment, or few segments) is about *niche* marketing; Tie Rack, Sock Shop and The Grateful Dead follow this approach. Jerry Garcia (of Grateful Dead) says, 'You do not merely want to be considered just the best of the best. You want to be considered the only ones who do what you do.'[5] The marketer who adopts a concentrated strategy concentrates on being the very best within a single tiny segment.

- *Differentiated* marketing (multisegmented) means concentrating on two or more segments, offering a differentiated marketing mix for each. Trust-house Forte runs the most prestigious hotels in the country, but also Motor Lodges at motorway services, with a different marketing strategy for each type of hotel. The hotels all carry the THF logo, even though the service levels and prices are different.

- *Undifferentiated* marketing is about using a 'scattergun' approach. Coca-Cola used to do this. The company had one product, one approach and one ad to appeal to all ages and shapes. The famous 'I'd like to teach the world to sing' campaign of the early 1970s was an example: a group of people of all ages and races stood on the side of a mountain singing, 'I'd like to buy the world a Coke'. In fact, Coca-Cola does appeal to a very wide range of ages and nationalities, which is somewhat unusual considering that most foods are strongly culturally linked.

The decision regarding which strategy to adopt will rest on the following three factors: the company's *resources*; the product *features and benefits*; and the *characteristics of the segment(s)*.Clearly if resources are limited, the company will tend to adopt a concentrated marketing approach. This is the approach taken by High and Mighty, the menswear retailer. This company specializes in clothing for exceptionally tall and exceptionally large men, and has become highly successful even though its market (men over 6' 4", or over 25 stone in weight) is actually small (numerically!) in absolute terms. The reason for the success is that men of this size are not catered for at all by the big chain retailers, and the alternative used to be to have everything tailor-made. High and Mighty is able to produce in sufficient quantities to keep prices reasonable (though still considerably higher than chain store prices), while still catering for its segment.

A higher level of resourcing coupled with a range of segments to approach will lead to a differentiated approach, and a simple made-for-everybody type of product will lead to an undifferentiated approach. Table 10.4 shows this in action. Companies with a small resource base are unable to attack large, mass markets simply because they cannot afford the level of promotional spend needed to make their voices heard above the big firms. They therefore need to differentiate, perhaps by starting out in a small area of the country and gradually spreading nationwide as resources become available.

Table 10.4 Effects of high- and low-level resourcing

Type of product	High-differentiation consumers	Low-differentiation consumers
High-resource company		
Mass market	Differentiated	Undifferentiated
Specialist market	Differentiated	Concentrated
Low-resource company		
Mass market	Concentrated	Differentiated (perhaps geographically)
Specialist market	Concentrated	Concentrated

Key points from this chapter

This chapter has been about dividing markets into groups with similar needs. The key points from the chapter are as follows:

- There are few, if any, mass markets left.
- If most consumers already own the core benefits of a product, the market must be segmented if success is to follow.
- Segments must be measurable, accessible, substantial and congruous.
- The profitability of a segment is calculated as the number of people in the segment multiplied by the premium they are willing to pay.
- The narrower the segment, the fewer the customers, but the greater the satisfaction and the greater the premium they are willing to pay.
- There are many ways to segment a market: in fact, as many ways as there are groups with congruent needs.
- The UK population is ageing rapidly due to low birth rate and greater longevity. This is affecting the size and nature of traditional segments.

Notes

1. Jan Larson, 'A segment of one', *American Demographics* (December 1991).
2. M.J. Evans, 'Domesday marketing?', *Journal of Marketing Management*, vol. 10, no. 5 (1991), pp. 409–31.
3. Paul Herbig, William Koehler and Ken Day, 'Marketing to the baby bust generation', *Journal of Consumer Marketing*, vol. 10, no 1 (1993), pp. 4–9.
4. James F. Engel, Roger D. Blackwell and Paul W. Miniard, *Consumer Behaviour*, 8th edn (Fort Worth, TX: Dryden Press, 1995), chapter 3.
5. *Ibid.*

11

Buyer behaviour in services markets

After reading this chapter, you should be able to:

- Explain the role of risk and uncertainty in service purchasing.
- Understand the importance of setting correct service levels.
- Handle post-purchase dissonance in service situations.
- Explain the key differences between services and physical products.

Services – products or not?

From the consumer's viewpoint a service is as much a bundle of benefits as is a physical product. The consumer is paying out hard-earned money for the purpose of getting something back; the fact that the product is not actually something that can be held in the hand is irrelevant.

For example, consider the difference between a pizza bought from Tesco's freezer counter, and one bought in a pizza restaurant. The Tesco's pizza will be pretty much identical to the one next to it in the rack, and may have been produced weeks beforehand; you may not consume it for several more weeks, if you are stocking up the freezer. As a consumer, you are buying the pizza so that you can have a convenient meal at some later date.

In the pizza restaurant, though, the benefits you gain go far beyond merely satisfying hunger. Often you will be with friends (or on a date), satisfying your social needs as well. The restaurant provides you with a pleasant atmosphere, does the washing-up for you, and even panders to your esteem needs by waiting on you. The actual pizza will vary from one customer to another – partly because the pizzas are made to order, and partly because the chef may not use exactly the same quantities of the various ingredients each time, or it may be a different chef each night. Clearly, though, the bulk of what you are paying for when you go to a restaurant is the *intangible* part of the deal: the atmosphere, the socializing, the attention of the waiter. The pizza is certainly part of it, but it probably represents less than 20 per cent of the final bill.

Usually services cannot be tested before you agree to purchase, because the only way to test is actually to use the service. For instance, when you buy the pizza from Tesco's you could take a good look at it first, read the ingredients list, and see if it looks like an appealing brand; however, if you do not like the waitress in the restaurant, this is difficult to complain about (unless there is something seriously wrong with the way you have been served). You can only pay up and smile, perhaps leaving a smaller tip than you had intended to. Refusal to pay afterwards only works if the service is very seriously poor.

From the supplier's viewpoint, a further problem is apparent. Services cannot be stockpiled in the same way as physical products. If the restaurant has a quiet night, the waiters and chefs still have to be paid; the service they would have provided has not been sold, but the cost of employing them remains. Conversely, if Tesco's does not sell the frozen pizza today, it can be sold tomorrow. Services are, therefore, highly perishable compared with physical products.

We can see, then, that services are distinguished from physical products by the following characteristics:

- They are intangible.
- Production and consumption usually happen at the same time.
- There is a lack of trialability.
- Services are variable, even from the same supplier.
- Services are perishable.

This naturally leads to problems for the consumer, since buying a service will inevitably look like buying a pig in a poke. In effect, consumers are buying a promise: the service provider is offering certain benefits which may or may not appear, and the consumer has little redress if the service does not come up to expectation.

We will now examine the purchasing process as it relates to services.

Consumer approaches to information gathering

In services markets, consumers rely much more on word of mouth than is the case with physical products. Because of the intangibility of the product, the consumer is unable to carry out many of the usual processes of information gathering – advertising is less verifiable, the suppliers are often unable to be specific about the service and the quality thereof, and most services are less subject to close regulation by government or trade bodies. Prospective consumers of a service are therefore likely to rely heavily on personal recommendations by friends and colleagues. This is particularly true of services such as hairdressing and restaurants.

For professional services, the consumer may also ask questions about the qualifications and credentials of the service provider. For example, a consumer who is looking for a solicitor to handle a divorce case will naturally want to seek out a specialist in family law, and will look into this aspect of the solicitor's experience. Professional services rely heavily on referrals from other professionals: estate agents recommend solicitors, who recommend accountants, and so forth.

Risk and uncertainty

Consumers will naturally want to minimize risk. Risk involves not only the possible loss of the purchase price of the product, but also some consequential losses. In the case of purchase of services, these consequential losses can be quite substantial: for example, poor legal advice could conceivably result in the loss of millions of pounds, or even one's liberty. Even the injudicious purchase of a restaurant meal could result in food poisoning. Table 11.1 illustrates some of the risks and the possible remedies.

Of course, there is a risk attached to the purchase of physical products as well, but usually the risk is confined to the purchase price (no doubt there are many exceptions to this general rule) and in the event of buying a faulty product, it is possible to obtain a replacement or a refund. Consumers therefore need to weigh up the purchase decision for both value for money (assuming the service that the consumer expects when agreeing to the purchase is what is actually obtained) and also the possible consequential loss if the service offering goes wrong. Because of the risk of consequential loss, consumers will frequently avoid the cheapest service, on the assumption that there 'must be something wrong with it'. Though this phenomenon is also noticeable for purchases of physical products, it is far more common with the purchase of services. For example, ladies' hairdressing is not price sensitive, and consumers often show perverse price sensitivity (deliberately going to a more expensive salon, all other aspects being equal).

Naturally, consumers will still expect to see value for money, having made the decision to opt for the higher-price alternative.

Table 11.1 Risks and remedies

Type of risk	Possible consumer response	Possible supplier remedy	Explanation
Consequential loss	Lawsuit	Ensure that risks are explained beforehand; use disclaimers in contracts; carry public or professional liability insurance	Consequential losses arise when a service goes wrong and causes damage to the customer. For example, if a train is late and the customer misses a vital business meeting, there may be a big consequential loss. British Rail has disclaimers on the back of the ticket for this type of loss.
Purchase price risk	Refuse to pay	Correct the fault; check with the customer during the service provision that everything is all right.	It is too late afterwards to ask if everything is all right (although this should be done). Checking during the service (a) makes it less likely that things will go wrong and (b) makes it harder for the consumer to claim that the service went wrong in order to avoid paying.
Misunderstanding about what was wanted	Complain, perhaps refuse to pay	Before providing the service, go through everything carefully and explain exactly what is going to be done, when and why. Perhaps even explain why the job cannot be done the way the consumer would like it to be done.	One of the commonest problems in service provision is lack of real communication. This is particularly true in professional services, where the professional perhaps rightly feels that the customer would not understand the finer technical details of the job. It is worthwhile providing an explanation, however, since there is otherwise a potential for post-purchase dissonance.

Consumers are faced with a greater degree of uncertainty when purchasing services, in that the service is (a) intangible and (b) variable. Even the supplier of the service cannot always guarantee that the outcome will be to the consumer's satisfaction; this is particularly true of professional services, such as lawyers and accountants. Lawyers still expect to be paid even if they lose the case, and likewise an accountant will still expect a fee even if the profit and loss account is not as healthy as the client would like, or the tax authorities do not allow all the deductions. Equally, if the restaurant is not as romantic as you had expected and your date is displeased, the waiter will still expect you to pay for the meal.

This is, of course, outside the scope of errors or misunderstandings. If you ordered a mild curry and got a spicy one instead, you have cause to complain; the problem arises when what is described to you in good faith turns out differently from what you expected. The uncertainty usually arises from the gap between what the consumer is expecting in the way of benefits, and what the service provider can actually provide.

For example, it is well known in ladies' hairdressing that some clients expect to come out looking like their favourite movie star or pop singer. While it is sometimes (though by no means always) possible to recreate the appropriate hairstyle, it is not possible to carry out plastic surgery, and the particular hairstyle may not suit the customer's facial or physical features. Not unnaturally, this causes post-purchase dissonance: either the stylist must explain to the customer why the hairstyle will not work, or the stylist has to reproduce the hairstyle and handle the customer's disappointment. There is more later on how to handle this kind of post-purchase dissonance.

Consumers may seek to reduce uncertainty by looking for guarantees from the service provider; unfortunately, since services are perishable and not reclaimable, the supplier is rarely able to recoup anything from a 'returned' service. This makes suppliers reluctant to offer money-back guarantees, and therefore the consumer would normally be faced with a greater level of uncertainty.

Purchase of a service differs slightly from purchase of a physical good. Typically, the purchase of a physical good follows the sequence shown in Figure 11.1. The fact that the service is frequently not paid for until after it has been delivered and consumed means that the consumer is offered a considerable degree of reassurance. Also, because the service is being consumed as it is being produced, the supplier and the consumer have ample opportunity to confirm that what is being supplied is meeting the consumer's expectations. This is why waiters will typically check with diners that their meals are OK: it reduces the risk that the consumer will complain after the meal has been consumed.

Reducing the risk for the consumer will, of course, increase it for the supplier. Suppliers often have problems with customers who do not pay up

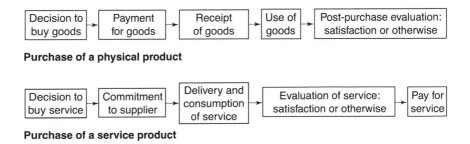

Figure 11.1 Comparison of purchase of physical products and services

on time, and it can be difficult for the supplier to recoup the loss; it is not possible to repossess a dinner for two or a haircut, and suing clients for non-payment for professional services such as accountancy can prove problematic, since the client can easily claim that the service was inadequate in some respect. Service industries tend to lose more money this way than physical product suppliers lose through pilfering.

Involvement

Because of the greater risks and uncertainty attached to purchase of services, consumers are likely to become more involved with the service provider, and therefore more brand loyal. In other words, having found a restaurant which provides a reliable meal in the right atmosphere, the consumer will tend to keep returning there rather than risk going somewhere new.

This is particularly true in the case of personal services, such as hairdressing. Loyalty to the service provider is extremely strong, because of the personal contact necessary for carrying out the service, and typically extends beyond loyalty to the salon. The loyalty is usually extended to the actual hairstylist providing the service. In many cases, the relationship between the hairstylist and the customer becomes a lifetime one, only breaking down when the hairstylist retires.

For comparison, consider how loyal the average motorist is to a car manufacturer. Despite car purchase being used by textbook authors as a prime example of a high-involvement purchase, most motorists will have tried several different manufacturers, and certainly many different models, over a lifetime's driving. It would be difficult for car manufacturers to find customers who *always* buy their brand; yet it has been fairly straightforward for Frizzell Insurance to find a group of customers who have *always* insured through the company, and Frizzell has successfully used these customers in its recent advertising campaigns.

This is true of most services, from restaurants to banking. Consumers are reluctant to switch bank accounts, even when problems become apparent with their current bankers; likewise people will tend to use the same solicitor rather than switch. For this reason, solicitors will tend to operate from practices large enough to accommodate the various specialist functions (family law, criminal law, conveyancing, etc.) because the client who originally came to the firm for a house purchase is likely to return when he needs defending on a drunk-driving charge, or needs to sue somebody for a debt.

Likewise, although consumers will readily switch brands of baked beans in order to get twopence off, they will buy the beans from their usual supermarket. This is because the consumer knows where everything is in the supermarket, knows what the store's policy is on returned goods, knows which credit cards are acceptable, knows what the store's own brands are like, and so on. Supermarkets worldwide have recently begun to encourage this by the use of loyalty or 'Club' cards.

The reason for this is not that the supermarkets have suddenly become aware of the involvement phenomenon, but rather that the technology of electronic point-of-sale (EPOS) equipment has become sophisticated enough to handle the amount of data involved. In future, the supermarkets will be able to keep complete records of each customer's buying pattern and act accordingly: for example, it would be quite feasible in future to remind customers at the checkout that they are running low on, say, tomato ketchup – and to know the brand and size that the customer usually buys.[1]

Sales promotion

Promotion schemes for services are therefore somewhat problematic: customers are less likely to switch merely because of a temporary price reduction or 'special offer'. It is possible, as we have seen, to encourage *existing* customers to stay (and in fact this is likely to be the most cost-effective way of doing business, as it is in the case of physical products), but it is harder to bring in new customers.

Typically, service providers focus on problems which they have identified with the competition. For example, some bank customers feel strongly about banks which invest in countries with oppressive regimes; the Co-operative Bank has been able to capitalize on this by promising that it will never do so. In this case the bank is playing off one involvement (with the customer's existing bank) against another (the customer's involvement with a social cause).

Likewise, First Direct has based its entire existence on the fact that most working people cannot get to a bank during normal banking hours; the bank has made deep inroads into the personal banking sector by offering 24-hour telephone banking.

Many service providers make good use of the consumer's need to belong by offering 'club' membership. This ranges from the 'exclusive flight deals' offered by RCI, the timeshare exchange company, through to the 'Friends of the Theatre' benefits offered by some theatres and theatrical companies. Museums and galleries often offer season tickets, as (of course) do transport services such as trains and buses.

Perhaps the biggest recent phenomenon in loyalty schemes for regular customers has been the frequent-flyer programmes, which began in the

USA during the late 1970s and early 1980s. Following the deregulation of US airspace, many companies sprang up to compete with the majors; routes were no longer the exclusive province of the big airlines, and the government-sanctioned monopolies no longer applied, with the result that fierce price wars broke out. Airlines which had previously not had to compete at all in any real sense suddenly found themselves scrambling for business; the result was a burgeoning frequent-flyer programme, by which airlines gave free flights to loyal customers.

This type of programme now exists among all the world's major airlines, and usually also covers 'associate' airlines: for example, United Airlines of the USA has a reciprocal agreement with local airline Ansett in Australia, with Aloha Airlines in Hawaii, British Midland in Europe, and several other local airlines worldwide. This ensures that customers flying with any of these airlines can still obtain frequent-flyer points for the entire journey, so that the airline prevents the competition from offering a more comprehensive route coverage and thus luring customers away. Each airline benefits, since they do not compete directly with each other; also the small airlines have a better chance of surviving in an industry dominated by the big players.

This type of loyalty programme should be distinguished from promotions such as air miles. Since air miles can be collected from a large number of outlets and suppliers, they cannot be considered as a loyalty programme; the air miles system is intended as a sales promotion exercise, to persuade customers to use one supplier rather than another.

Service levels

The service level refers to the degree to which the customer's needs are met. For example, an airline might aim for a service level criterion of ensuring that 95 per cent of flights leave within ten minutes of the scheduled time. Or perhaps a pizza delivery service might guarantee that pizzas will be delivered within thirty minutes, or the pizza is free. (This particular type of guarantee was outlawed in Dublin because it resulted in too many road accidents caused by over-hasty pizza delivery drivers.)

The UK government's recent efforts to establish Citizen's Charters for the various government departments is an example of trying to improve service levels. In effect, there has been a recognition that taxpayers are actually paying for a service, and that the Inland Revenue, DSS, Customs and Excise, National Health and other departments are there to provide that service. Clearly it cannot always be the case that the service is provided to the complete satisfaction of the client (nobody is happy to pay the Inland

Revenue), but at least the service can be run in a sympathetic way that minimizes inconvenience to the customer.

Here are some recent examples of firms seeking to raise service levels:

- British Rail Intercity aims to ensure that 90 per cent of trains arrive within ten minutes of the scheduled time, and that 99 per cent of services will run.
- Tesco's guarantees that, if there is one other person in front of you, it will open another checkout, unless all the checkouts are open already.
- Do It All provides special advisers to guide customers through the technicalities of DIY jobs, and to advise on which products will be best for the job.
- Post Office Counters guarantee that 95 per cent of clients will be dealt with within five minutes.

The decision about service levels will depend mainly on economic factors and the value-for-money perception of the clients. This reverts back to the problem examined earlier, that clients will often pay more for a service because they believe that this will mean, in itself, that they will get a better service; disappointment may creep in afterwards. Put another way, a consumer who is paying £100 a night to stay in a five-star hotel will expect the room service to be comprehensive, polite, and prompt. The same consumer staying in Mrs Boggins' bed and breakfast for £12 a night will not expect any room service at all. Conversely, small B & B guest houses have a reputation for providing a good, filling, old-fashioned British breakfast, and guests will be expecting this as part of the service.

The service level must relate to something that the customer feels is important. Saying that you will ensure that shopping trolleys are returned to the pick-up point within ten minutes of the previous customers abandoning them at the other end of the car park is unlikely to be of much help to the customer. Saying that you will guarantee never to be out of stock of certain essential items is probably far more relevant.

Likewise the service level set must be within your powers to achieve. Guaranteeing sunshine for a holiday-maker is clearly beyond the control of the tour operator (but a cash rebate for every day when the sun does not shine is within the supplier's control, and might be highly relevant).

It is important to understand here that the service level must be *appropriate* to meet expectations, not at the *maximum*. A consumer paying a low price will be expecting drawbacks: cheapskates do not expect to be looked after very well, and may become suspicious if the service is too good. In other words, it is possible to make your customers think that there must be a catch somewhere.

The early experience of Safeway supermarkets in the UK markets bore this out. In the USA, Safeway (in common with most other supermarkets) employs packers to pack customers' purchases into carrier bags, and even carry the bags to the customer's car (usually in the expectation of a tip). There is no charge for this service. When Safeway entered the UK market, the company followed the same practice, but UK shoppers (who are not used to this level of service) became suspicious and assumed that the shop's prices must be higher in order to pay for the higher service level. Safeway eventually discontinued the practice, although packers are still available on request.

Likewise, customers shopping at discount stores such as Kwiksave expect that the goods will be less attractively displayed and that the checkout queues will be longer. The store management deliberately keep the surroundings less attractive than the mainstream supermarkets so that the customer's perception is that the prices *must* be much lower. Aldi, on the other hand, maintain a pleasant shopping environment while still keeping prices extra-low; this may, in the long run, prove counterproductive as it runs counterperceptive. Watch this space!

To sum up this section, the main decision criteria regarding service levels are as follows:

- The service level must relate to a benefit the customer feels is important.
- The service level must be achievable.
- It must be appropriate rather than optimal.

Handling dissonance

Of course, sometimes things go wrong and the customer is not happy with what has been provided. In other words, what was delivered is not what was expected, and the service provider has to attempt to make amends in some way. As we have seen, consumers will tend to express their dissatisfaction in one of three ways:[2]

- Voice responses, in which the customer comes back and complains.
- Private responses, which would include telling friends about the poor service.
- Third-party responses, such as taking legal action.

The majority of service providers try to ensure that this does not happen, by using the following methods:

- Explaining the service in great detail beforehand and explaining what the possible drawbacks might be.

- Checking with the client during the provision of the service that everything is satisfactory.

An example of the first type of dissonance-reduction technique would be the initial consultation with a lawyer regarding a court case. The lawyer will typically warn the client that the outcome of any court case cannot be guaranteed, that the client may incur substantial court (and lawyer) costs without actually winning the case, that the opposition may come up with some line of defence (or attack, as the case may be) which is unanticipated, and so on.

An example of the second approach would be in an aircraft first-class cabin, where the flight attendants check regularly with the passengers to ensure that all is well. This approach is often used where the service is carried out over a period of time and the client is present throughout the service provision: medical procedures, air travel, hairdressing, beauty treatments, etc.

It is always worthwhile checking that the client fully understands what is being provided, whether the supplier is a doctor explaining the prognosis for a surgical operation, or a waiter explaining that the dish being ordered is extra-spicy. This is why detailed descriptions of ingredients, and even the cooking instructions, are usually given on restaurant menus.

Even so, things can go wrong, sometimes because the variability of the service leads to a failure to provide the service at the level expected. Even the service provider can be surprised at the outcome in these cases.

The remedy has, of course, to fit the circumstances. Because the customer's loss falls into two categories – loss of the service and consequential loss – it may be necessary to lay down specific rules beforehand to limit the supplier's liability.[3] For example, photographic development services usually limit their liability to the cost of a new roll of film. This means that they can avoid the possibility of being sued for loss of, say, irreplaceable wedding photographs or holiday snaps.

Services fall into the following categories, for the purpose of correcting complaints:

- Services where it is appropriate to offer a repeat service, or a voucher. Examples are dry cleaners, domestic appliance repairers and takeaway food outlets.
- Services where giving the money back will usually be sufficient. Examples are retail shops, cinemas and theatres and video rental companies.
- Services where consequential losses may have to be compensated for. Examples are medical services, solicitors and hairdressers.

The above categorizations are not necessarily exclusive, in the sense that it may be true to say that *most* times giving disappointed theatre-goers their money back is sufficient, but sometimes they may sue for travelling costs (or even for injury, in the event of an accident during a performance). For this reason, service providers usually carry public liability insurance, and the third category of service providers usually also have professional liability insurance which covers for consequential losses.

Unlike compensation for the failure of a physical product, it is often difficult to quantify an appropriate level of compensation for a failed service. For example, if a new personal stereo breaks down in the first week, it can be replaced with an identical model or the customer's money can be returned. If, however, a perm is not quite tight enough for the client, a repeat service may not be possible (due to the risk of overprocessing the hair) and clearly the service is only a partial failure. In this case, returning the money may be an overcompensation, but something still needs to be done. These situations require careful judgement as to the degree of the client's dissatisfaction, and the best way of compensating the client; this will often require some skilful negotiation, and will be best carried out by somebody with a high level of authority.

Because service provision relies heavily on word-of-mouth, it is even more important that complaints are dealt with to the complete satisfaction of the customer than would be the case with physical products. As with physical products, consumers tend to be more prone to use negative word-of-mouth than positive word-of-mouth, but complaints correctly handled will generate more positive word-of-mouth than will a good service in itself. This means that a dissatisfied customer who is pleased with the compensation offered will be more likely to speak positively of the service provider than would a customer whose expectations had been met in the first place. (See Chapter 3 for a more complete discussion of post-purchase dissonance.)

For this reason, it is important to ensure that dissatisfied customers voice their dissatisfaction, and that the service provider answers the problem effectively. Airlines, tour operators and theatres frequently ask consumers to fill in market research questionnaires to determine satisfaction levels for various aspects of the service provision, but this is somewhat harder to do for restaurants and personal services; here it is more usual to rely on discussion between the service provider and the customer, rather than formal research.

Key points from this chapter

This chapter has been about consumer attitudes towards service provision. The key points from the chapter are as follows:

- A service is as much a product as is a physical item, even though it cannot be handled; this is because a service provides a bundle of benefits to the consumer, in exchange for payment.
- Consumers rely much more on word-of-mouth when choosing services, and will be more prone to using word-of-mouth after purchasing a service – whether to praise or condemn.
- Consumer risk is greater when buying a service than when buying a physical product, particularly as regards consequential losses.
- Some of this risk is reduced because consumers usually pay for services after consuming them.
- Consumers tend to be more loyal to service providers than to physical product suppliers, because there is often greater involvement.
- Sales promotion schemes tend to focus on comparisons with the competition, rather than on 'money off' deals.
- Service levels need to be appropriate, not optimal.
- Dissonance can be reduced by careful prior explanation of the service, and by monitoring during consumption.
- It is worthwhile encouraging customers to express dissatisfaction, rather than waiting for them to use word-of-mouth to damage your business.

Notes

1. Adrian Payne, *The Essence of Services Marketing*, (Hemel Hempstead: Prentice Hall, 1993).
2. Jagdip Singh, 'Consumer complaint intentions and behavior: definitions and taxonomical issues', *Journal of Marketing*, vol. 52 (January 1988), pp. 93–107.
3. Ralph L. Day, Klaus Brabicke, Thomas Schaetzle and Fritz Staubach, 'The hidden agenda of consumer complaining', *Journal of Retailing*, vol. 57 (Fall 1981), pp. 86–106.

12

Consumer behaviour in the marketing mix

After reading this chapter, you should be able to:

- Explain how marketers can plan strategies around consumer behaviour.
- Describe how consumer behaviour theory works in practice.
- Develop tactical methods for approaching markets.
- Understand how consumer attitudes can be changed.

Introduction

Most of this book has examined the theories behind consumer behaviour and the surrounding environmental issues that determine why people act in the ways they do in purchasing and consumption situations. Ultimately, though, marketers must develop strategies and tactics for launching products and expanding markets, and must therefore use the knowledge of how consumers approach purchasing decisions in order to achieve marketing objectives.

As a starting point, here are some of the factors that arise from the four Ps of marketing: price, product, place and promotion.

Price

As we saw in Chapter 9, consumers are often prepared to pay a premium price for something that fits their needs better than the product they currently use. When setting prices, the marketer needs to be in line with what the customer is prepared to pay or reasonably expects to pay; this bears no relation to the firm's costs in manufacturing the product.

Many companies still operate on a cost-plus pricing scheme. This means that the firm adds up what it costs to make the product, then adds on an amount for its profit, and sets the resulting total as the price. From a consumer's viewpoint this will hardly ever result in the price being 'correct', because the consumer is only interested in the value-for-money attributes of the product, not in the manufacturer's cost base. Either the price will be higher than the consumer thinks is reasonable, in which case the product will stay on the shelf, or it will be less than the consumer was expecting and he or she might become suspicious and think there is a catch, or a hidden drawback. At the very least, the company will give away profit which it could otherwise have made.

For this reason marketers should normally use *demand pricing*: in other words, price according to the expectations of the consumer.

Consumers shop around, but it is a rare consumer who always buys the cheapest product on offer. Generally speaking, consumers look for the best deal they can get consistent with meeting their needs, and will undertake a certain amount of searching to ensure this is so. For some consumers there is a hedonic element within the search process: most people love to find a bargain, which may be due to our hunter-gatherer ancestry.

The degree to which the search is worthwhile in terms of the practical aspects of the product is called the *functional approach*: in this case, obtaining the product at the lowest price. Cognition is the key to this. The search itself may also have hedonic aspects, and affect is more likely to be relevant here. On the other hand, there may be a hedonic benefit in paying a high price for a product. This can come about either because the individual feels this action will impress somebody else or because it just feels good to spend a large amount of money without having to think too much about it. It might be risky for a marketer to rely on this for a market, since such impulses are somewhat unpredictable.

The most important aspect of pricing strategy is to find out what the target market will think of as a reasonable price for the product, and for this reason much market research is concerned with finding out what value consumers would place on a product.

Product

A product is a bundle of benefits which goes far beyond the physical item itself. The physical features and use/benefit aspects are based on the consumer's cognitive processes, but the following are predicated by affect and conation:

- *Designer branding*. This can increase the observability of the product and raise the consumer's status with friends and others.
- *Styling*. The appearance of the product adds to the hedonic aspects of it, and also increases the observability.
- *Location/distribution* method. This can be important for conation: a consumer is more likely to espouse a particular type of purchase behaviour if the distribution method makes it convenient to do so. Also, the ambiance of the retail outlet can add to the hedonic aspects of the purchase.
- *Manufacturer's reputation*. This is certainly part of the affective component of purchase as well as the cognitive. Consumers will often become involved with a particular manufacturer.
- *Image of the product category/brand*. This is affective as well as cognitive.

Since people are often rationalizing rather than rational, these factors may play a much bigger part than the cognitive aspects. Harley-Davidson, along with other major motorcycle manufacturers, knows that it is selling mainly on a self-image platform; most bikers are in their forties or fifties. In fact, Harley says that it is competing with home extensions and new kitchens for the consumer's dollars. Middle-aged men buy high-performance motorbikes because they can afford the bike and afford the insurance, and they are reliving a dream of youth; this has virtually nothing to do with the need for transport that is the motorbike's original *raison d'être*.

The benefits that the consumer gains from buying a product relate to self-image, self-esteem and aesthetic needs, not purely the utilitarian aspects of the product. Marketers should look at the product in the light of the needs of the target market, and add value in ways other than the purely practical.

Place

This goes beyond mere convenience. Sometimes the place is part of the product, in the sense that there are benefits attaching to the place utility of the distribution. For example, consider the purchasing of antiques. Some antique buyers will scour car-boot sales, house clearance sales, auction rooms and the like in the hope of picking up a bargain. Others will go to antique shops where most of the searching has already been done; still others will visit upmarket antique galleries, where the pieces will be artfully displayed and the customer will be offered a glass of wine and a canapé while browsing.

In the course of an antique's passage from car-boot sale to upmarket dealer, the price may have risen from £3 to £2,000, yet at each stage of the process the purchaser has bought a bargain. The reason is that the location is part of the product. The bargain-hunter at the car-boot sale is prepared to spend days or weeks looking for that elusive bargain; the hedonic aspects of the search add to the joy of finding the appropriate product. At the end of the chain, the wealthy collector enjoying the glass of wine in the antique gallery is also enjoying the pleasure of having somebody explain the history and details of manufacture of the antique, and is about to invest a large amount of money in something that will hold its value and be a joy to own. The wealthy collector also gains the reassurance that the product will be the genuine article, and has the reputation of the gallery to back this up.

Buying goods from a catalogue, or from a street market, or from a department store each has its hedonic aspects; marketers need to balance the place utility (cognitive) aspects against the hedonic (affective) aspects of the point of purchase.

Promotion

This is the most visible area of marketing, and the one that most actively tries to tap into the consumer's decision-making processes. Promotion is about communicating with the consumer, and about persuading people to try our products, and is often very much concerned with attitude change.

Because attitudes are learned, promotional activities can offer new information to the consumer. Although the consumer's knowledge of the product is based on experience, this experience can be vicarious rather than personal: for example, by observing a model using the product.

The promotional mix splits into four subheadings.

Sales promotion is about making temporary increases in the sales of the product. A promotion might be a money-off deal, a free gift, a free sample of the product, a two-for-the-price-of-one offer, or a competition or lottery. Sales promotions frequently act as an interrupt: the consumer notices the special offer while browsing or looking for something else entirely, and is diverted temporarily. Money-off deals appeal to the consumer through cognition, but also appeal to the hedonistic desire to get a bargain. Having been interrupted, the consumer will usually return to the original activity.

The free trial-size pack is useful for improving the consumer's learning experience of the product, provided the consumer actually uses the product as a result of being given the pack. Many trial packs are simply discarded. Such promotions work best when the consumer is asked to comment on the experience of using the product. For example, a trial visit to a timeshare complex is more effective if the consumer is asked questions about the experience, or is asked to complete a questionnaire. This is a form of operant conditioning, and can be a very effective way of marketing an unsought good of this nature. Operant conditioning can also be used to encourage consumers to respond to mailshots and press ads; insurance companies now frequently offer free gifts to those who respond to such advertising.

Sales promotion is of most use during the beginning of the adoption process, but a good sales promotion can be used at any stage of the product life cycle. In terms of the *AIDA* model, the promotion is intended to catch the consumer's attention and arouse interest; the product itself should create the desire for a repeat purchase, and thus the action of buying. The more complex *hierarchy of effects* model begins with knowledge about the product, which is best obtained by use of a free sample. If the product is innovative, there is scope for aiming the sales promotion at the innovators among the consumers, since these are likely to be influential in the long run.

The second element of the promotional mix is *advertising*. Advertising is a paid communication placed in a medium, and is probably the most visible of the marketing tools available. Advertising is also one of the most important methods by which marketers try to educate consumers about their products, and can be broadly categorized as in Table 12.1.

In most advertising, the use of the one-sided message is the norm: only the positive aspects of the product are given, not the negatives. This can result in mistrust by consumers, since the message is biased. Many advertisers think that a two-sided message is risky, since the marketer will not be able to argue the case for the positive aspects in person, and therefore the consumer may accept the negatives and ignore the positives. However, there is some evidence to show that this is not always the case.

For example, if the audience is already critical towards the product, the marketer has nothing to lose by admitting that there are drawbacks to the product, and has the opportunity to meet criticisms head on and provide a counterargument. Second, if the audience is intelligent, the marketer will gain credibility by being honest. Research has also shown that the two-sided approach results in the advertisement being remembered longer.[1]

Frequency of exposure to an advertisement is a major issue, since there is an assumption that the more times the consumer sees the ad, the stronger will be the learning experience. There is evidence that boredom sets in after around fifteen exposures[2] and the consumer begins to form a negative opinion of the product simply through finding the repeated advertisement irritating. Unfortunately, this tends to militate against the classical conditioning approach described in Chapter 4.

Advertising has the drawback that the communication is one-way, and cannot give feedback or positive reinforcement of consumer actions. For this to happen, it is necessary to use *personal selling*.

Personal selling is the process whereby a salesperson interacts with a potential customer with the objective of achieving a sale. Salespeople usually begin by finding out what the customer needs, then present a

Table 12.1 Examples of types of advertising appeal

Type of appeal of advert	Example	Explanation	Tactical approach
Hedonic	Cadbury's Caramel: the female hare relaxing with the chocolate bar	The ad is emphasizing the pleasurable aspects of using the product, rather than the practicalities. For products such as chocolate, this is almost the only available appeal, since there is no real nutritional argument in favour of eating chocolate.	The emphasis needs to be on the 'go on, spoil yourself' type of appeal. This is particularly so for products which are deemed to be unhealthy but fun, such as chocolate, cream cakes and burgers. A visit to McDonald's 'makes your day'; the advertising does not emphasize that McDonald's provides you with a quick lunch for £3.50.
Cognitive appeal	Recent VW Polo ads, where the boyfriend cannot believe the car is so cheap, and thinks his girlfriend must have earned the money for it in an illicit manner	The ad is humorous, but makes the point that the consumer can buy a lot of car for a little money.	Here the appeal is to the consumer's practical sensibilities. The car has a reputation for being reliable and well made, and this has fed over into a view that it must therefore be expensive. A superstitious belief has grown up, and the ad is intended to counteract that by presenting new information, and thus changing the perceptions of the consumer.
Classical conditioning	Levi's ad featuring the 'Spaceman' music	The association of the song with the product means that the product will come to mind whenever the song is played.	The song and the product should be presented together as often as possible. The song should not be released into the record shops until each potential consumer has had enough exposures to the ad to establish the conditioned reflex. If possible, the song should be played in the retail outlets as well.
Family decision-making units	The Bold ad, where the teenager is sent to buy washing powder and fabric conditioner and saves money by buying the Bold	This ad taps into the growing phenomenon of young teen and pre-teen family purchasing. Because so many parents work, the children of the family are often delegated as purchasing agents. The ad appeals to those children who are sent shopping, by showing a peer carrying out a complex search and decision process.	For this type of approach to work, the ad must show a credible role-model. This will usually be an older teenager, and the behaviour must appear to be rewarded by the parent in a credible way. Showing the teenager as being empowered in the purchasing situation is also important, since we would like our target audience to act in this way when sent to do the shopping.

New product launches	The First Direct adverts, which invited customers to switch TV channel to see the rest of the information	The ads aroused people's interest because they required the audience to change channels in order to see the full ad. By getting people to do something, the bank increased the customer's involvement in the learning process. This is almost a form of operant conditioning. It also tended to separate out those who had remote control for their TVs from those who did not.	The approach of this series of ads was innovative, and therefore appealed to innovators. The innovators would be those who were dissatisfied with their existing banks and would be interested enough to go to the trouble of switching channels.
Teaser campaigns	The recent series of Going Places billboard ads, showing people with various problems (Get rid of dirty floors for two weeks!) without actually showing the product name	The teaser campaign operates by arousing the customer's interest and curiosity; the teaser is shown for a month or so, then the denouement reveals the name of the product. Teasers induce interest and awareness; trial and adoption need to be addressed by sales promotion techniques.	Teaser campaigns will only work for new products, and especially for new companies entering a market. They have been used successfully by Elf Aquitaine entering the UK market, and for launches of new films. The critical aspect of teaser campaigns is to get the timing right between teaser and denouement: too short and the consumer's curiosity will not have been aroused, too long and the ad will have become 'part of the furniture' and the point will be lost.
Aspirational reference group	Nescafé Gold Blend, which has been showing a long-running 'soap opera' romance between an attractive, successful couple. The series of ads is now on its second couple, and is used worldwide.	The appeal of the ad is based on the aspirational reference group for the target market. A large number of consumers wish they were attractive, romantic and successful, and the implication of the ad is that people in that group are the ones who drink Gold Blend.	Lifestyle advertising almost always uses the aspirational reference group for its appeal. The aim is to ensure that the people shown in the ad really do represent the reference group, and also that the reference group identified is one that the consumers will aspire to.
Dissociative reference groups	A counter-approach to the aspirational group advertising has been used by Audi, where the ad shows a somewhat ruthless go-getting young man taking the car for a test drive and then saying it's not really his style.	Because the young man comes across as being a rather unpleasant, 1980s-style yuppie, the consumer feels drawn to the car by negative association.	The danger with this type of ad is that the consumer may not always follow the ad through to the last frame, where it becomes clear that the unpleasant character actually does not want the car. Usually this type of approach works best when combined with the aspirational group; showing somebody from the aspirational group using the product would improve the impact of the ad.
Psychoanalytic or Freudian ads	Peugeot car ad, in which a man takes a sexy-looking woman for a drive which ends with a seduction on a beach (the woman later turns out to be his wife)	The advert associates sex with the car, in a fairly obvious way. The implication is that, although it is a family car, it is still sexy and sporty. The appeal is to the id rather than the ego.	This type of approach is frequently used in car ads, and seems to work best on men. The ads need to be tastefully produced, and will often also have an appeal based on an aspirational group (particularly as most people's real lives are seldom as romantic).

Table 12.2 Examples of sales statements

Salesperson's statement	Explanation
'We find that most people prefer the tilt-and-turn handles. How do you feel about them?'	Here the salesperson is using *normative compliance* to encourage the customer to agree. This type of question is less a request for information, and more a way of leading the customer to the sale.
'They'll look good when they're fitted, won't they?'	This rhetorical question operates on three fronts: first, the *abstract goal* of impressing the neighbours by having smart new windows; second, by using the *value-expressive influence* of showing that the consumer cares about his/her home; third, the question uses *normative compliance* because it assumes that the consumer is going to buy the windows. It is possible that, for some consumers, the question triggers their *aesthetic* needs.
'I expect you'll be glad not to have to paint the windows ever again.'	This appeal works on the *cognitive* aspect of the consumer's attitude to the product by showing a practical reason for buying.
'If we can get on with the paperwork tonight, I can offer you an extra discount. It's just our way of thanking you for not making me waste time calling back!'	It is common to offer an incentive to the customer to agree to the sale on the same night as the presentation. This can take the form of an extra discount, or sometimes a free gift; it appeals to the customer's need to save time in making an external *information search* by justifying going ahead now. The salesperson will usually 'dress up' the offer rather more than as shown here!

possible solution to the problem, then use one of a selection of possible closes to secure the sale.

Salespeople use a series of techniques to lead the customer to a buying decision, beginning with opening techniques. Here the salesperson is asking questions to activate the consumer's needs; Table 12.2 gives some examples, taken from a double-glazing presentation.

Salespeople will usually avoid asking questions to which there is a 'no' answer, even when not directly related to the sale. This is because they want the prospective customer to be in the mood to say 'yes' when the final question ('Will you buy the product?') is asked. This is an example of *classical conditioning*. Normative compliance is frequently used in the salesperson's body language – when the salesperson nods, the customer nods, and so forth. Table 12.3 shows some techniques for handling objections.

Salespeople develop a large armoury of techniques for persuading consumers to buy. In fact, these techniques are mainly aimed at leading the customer through the decision-making process by establishing or activating a need, supplying the relevant information, overcoming objections and helping the consumer to evaluate the product, and finally using a closing

Table 12.3 Objection handling techniques

Objection	Salesperson's response	Explanation
'I'll have to see my bank manager about the money.'	'Fine. Would you mind if our finance people consider you for a loan while you're considering them?'	This sets up an alternative which may save the customer time on the information search.
'I never buy anything on credit.'	'That's fine. We certainly don't mind being paid cash! But I assume you bought the rest of the house on a mortgage? So why not the windows?'	Here the customer has established a decision rule which the salesperson is trying to show has already been broken. It is difficult to attack a decision rule head on; it would be better to find out whether the rule is *compensatory* or *non-compensatory* first, to see whether it can be outweighed.
'I would like to see other companies' products before I decide.'	'Fine! Let me show you some of their samples, then you decide.'	Here the consumer is trying to establish a *consideration set* and the salesperson is trying to ensure that the set is established from information supplied by his/her own company.
'It's rather expensive – more than I really wanted to pay.'	'Well, you get what you pay for, I'm afraid – and a wrong decision now could mean you're living with cheap, ugly windows for an awfully long time.'	The salesperson is giving a *signal* that the high price relates to the high quality of the windows. Also, the salesperson is activating the *social risk* fear in the consumer by implying that the cheap windows might not look good.

technique to bring the prospect to the point of purchase. Salespeople cannot make people buy things they do not want; they can only try to introduce new information to change attitudes, then work through the decision-making process with the consumer to reach a decision.

Another element in the promotional mix is *public relations*, or PR. PR is about creating favourable attitudes among the organization's publics, and relies heavily on affect. A firm's PR activities will be either *reactive* (responding to customer complaints or adverse publicity) or *proactive* (organizing events or press releases that enhance the company image).

PR works by changing the audience's *salient beliefs* about the organization. In the case of reactive PR, the organization will try to set up a counterargument to the one being put forward by its detractors. For example, when McDonald's was accused of being environmentally unsound and contributing to the destruction of the tropical rainforests by encouraging greater beef production in South America, the company responded by pointing out that all its burgers are sourced locally in each country that it operates in. The company went on to point out that it uses recycled paper containers, and employs a litter patrol at each restaurant to collect any discarded packaging.

In the case of proactive PR, the organization tries to establish a favourable view among consumers by putting forward a positive view of its activities. This is done by appealing to the cognitive aspects of the consumers' attitude, usually by issuing press releases. A press release is more likely to be read and believed by consumers than is an advertisement, because it appears in the body of the news stories within the newspaper or other medium. The intention of PR is not to develop a *conation* regarding a product; it is merely to develop a positive *affect* through the audience's *cognition* about the company.

Consumer research

Any marketing decision making must always begin with the consumer. Because the consumer's purchase is the result of an interaction between the firm's activities and the consumer's demography, psychology and sociological characteristics, it is clearly essential for the firm to understand the consumer. Research may be conducted for any of the following reasons:

- To understand which types of people would be the best customers for the product.
- To find out what it is about our product that is discouraging some people from buying it.
- To find out which products we could produce that would fit consumers' needs better than what is already on the market.
- To find out which promotional methods would most appeal to the people we hope will buy the product.

Researchers have a number of techniques at their disposal, but they will broadly have two main aims: to discover consumers' *attitudes*, or to discover their *behaviour*. Discovering behaviour further divides into two categories: discovering what the consumer's past behaviour has been, which can usually be easily found out through surveys, and discovering what a consumer's future behaviour might be, which is rather harder to determine.

Surveys are typically conducted by inviting consumers to fill in *questionnaires*, or by using *structured interviews*, to find out what their past purchasing behaviour has been. A self-completion questionnaire which asks the consumer to state which brand of chocolate he or she last bought, or which asks where he or she shops most frequently, is relatively easy to construct and complete, and will give reliable answers. This type of research can be analyzed to give numerical data, and is therefore called *quantitative* research. Questions which ask about future behaviour (for example, asking if the consumer would use a new shopping centre) are rather harder to construct and are certainly harder for the respondent to answer. For these issues, it is usually better to use motivational research techniques such as *focus groups* (as described in Chapter 3). This type of *qualitative* research will often give the researcher a clear idea of the dimensions of the problem: the areas of interest for the consumer, the areas where problems will arise, and so on. They will not easily be analyzed to give numerical data, so they are more often used to determine the qualities of the problem.

Another method of determining consumer behaviour is to observe. *Observation* methods will, again, provide qualitative data. For example, a toy company might observe how children respond to a new toy by simply allowing them to play with it and noting their reactions. Direct observation by researchers has the advantage that it does not rely on the consumer's faulty memory or desire to impress the interviewer.[3] Unfortunately, it is often costly and time consuming compared with questionnaires.

Determining possible future behaviour can sometimes be achieved by experiments. For example, a researcher may carry out a test marketing exercise. Here the product is launched in a small area of the country, and consumer responses to it are gauged before the product is released nationally. This method is often used for testing new advertising campaigns, or new fast-moving consumer goods such as biscuits or sweets. The biggest drawback of test marketing is that it allows competitors to rush through their own copycat versions of the product.

For determining attitudes, researchers will sometimes use focus groups or in-depth interviews. This is because people sometimes find it difficult to express attitudes about sensitive subjects, and also it is often hard for the researchers to devise suitable questions to tease out attitudes. In the case of hidden attitudes, the researcher might be able to use a projective technique: this involves, for example, showing the person a cartoon and asking him or her to say what the people are saying.

In Figure 12.1 the researcher is trying to find out what the person's attitude is to dating agencies. The respondent will actually write in what he or she would think in those circumstances, but will not have the psychological pressure of having to state his or her own, perhaps embarrassing, attitude.

The design and execution of research are critical to its reliability. Ensuring that the questions being asked actually do address the problem, that the questions can and will be answered honestly, and that the right group of consumers are being studied are only some of the problems inherent in consumer research.

These people have just been introduced through a dating agency. What do you think each one is thinking?

Figure 12.1 Projective technique

Marketing in the twenty-first century

The changing social paradigm has already been mentioned in earlier chapters. Combined with changes in the structure of families, the rise in environmentalism and the increasing crowding of the planet, the trend towards *inner direction* will lead the following effects to become apparent:

- There will be more independent travel, fewer package tours.
- Fewer collective entertainments (e.g. working men's clubs), more individual entertainments (computer games, video).
- More single-portion recipe products, fewer family-size packs.
- More solo sports such as tennis and badminton, fewer team sports such as football and rugby.
- More emphasis on mom-and-pop businesses, less emphasis on chains or franchises.
- Fewer cars, more bicycles.
- More bedsitters, fewer family homes.
- More vegetarians, fewer carnivores.

By 2012 around 30 per cent of European Union citizens will be vegetarians, the biggest category of households will be single-person, and the old socioeconomic methods of segmenting consumers will no longer be usable in the face of *downgrading* (deliberately seeking a job at a lower level to avoid stress) and self-actualisation activities.[4]

Conversely, the capability for measuring consumer behaviour and attitudes will be much greater, given the new technology of loyalty cards and EPOS records. Therefore, although in some respects uncertainty will increase for marketers, in other respects it will reduce.

Customer care and service levels

Ultimately the consumer is king. There is no future for a firm that does not take care of its customers, and the old-style firms which believe that they need only produce a good product at a low price will not survive in the twenty-first century.

Here are some tips for customer care:

- If you do not look after your customers, somebody else will.
- It is always cheaper to keep an existing customer than to find a new one.
- Complaints, if properly handled, actually increase the loyalty of the customer.
- Everybody would like to have a 'friend who's in the business'. Try to be that friend.
- People are not stupid and do not like being treated as if they were.
- Nobody buys anything they do not want.
- Smile!

Without customers there is no business. Theodore Levitt said: 'The purpose of a business is to create and keep a customer.' The whole basis of marketing is to put the customer at the centre of all activities; this is really the only logical approach to the problem of consumer choice. As long as consumers have choice, and as long as the world operates in an economy of plenty, consumer behaviour will be of paramount importance to marketers.

Key points from this chapter

This chapter has been about the ways in which marketers can adapt their approaches to take account of consumer behaviour. Here are the key points from the chapter:

- The right price is always the price that consumers see as good value for money; the firm's costs bear no relation to the correct price.
- The place where the product is purchased is also part of the bundle of benefits making up the product.
- Promotion must be geared to the consumer's aspirations, personality and needs.

- Products are only of interest to consumers for the benefits, both physical and psychological, that they bring.
- Without customers, there can be no business.

Notes

1. Linda L. Golden and Mark I. Alpert, 'Comparative analysis of the relative effectiveness of one- and two-sided communication for contrasting products', *Journal of Advertising*, vol. 16, no. 1 (1987), pp. 18–25.
2. Marian C. Burke and Julie A. Edell, 'Ad reactions over time: capturing changes in the real world', *Journal of Consumer Research*, vol. 13 (June 1986), pp. 114–18.
3. William D. Wells and Leonard A. Lo Sciuto, 'Direct observation of purchasing behaviour', *Journal of Marketing Research*, vol. 3 (August 1966), pp. 227–33.
4. J.W.D. Blythe, 'Twenty years on – Europe after 2012', *Journal of Marketing Management*, vol. 9 (January 1993), pp. 79–86.

Index